AGENDA FOR BIBLICAL PEOPLE

AGENDA FOR BIBLICAL PEOPLE

Jim Wallis

HARPER & ROW, PUBLISHERS

NEW YORK

HAGERSTOWN

SAN FRANCISCO

LONDON

Acknowledgment is made for permission to quote from the following:

Christ and the Powers by H. Berkhof, translated from the Dutch by John H. Yoder. Copyright 1962 by Mennonite Publishing House, Scottdale, Pa.

Library of Congress Cataloging in Publication Data

Wallis, Jim.
   Agenda for Biblical people.
   Bibliography: p.
   1. Christianity—20th century. 2. Church and the world. I. Title.
BR121.2.W25 1976   209'.04   75–36745
ISBN 0–06–069236–7 pbk.

77 78 79 80 81 10 9 8 7 6 5 4 3

To those with whom I am learning to
share my life and without whose encouragement this
book never would have been written.

Contents

Preface

I remember my own "conversion" as a six-year-old child, scared to death by a Sunday night evangelist who told us kids that the Lord would come to take our parents to heaven, away from us, and that I would be sent to a terrible place alone. That prospect caused me to repent of the sin and degradation of my first six years, and I was "saved." The call to costly discipleship wasn't raised that night, nor would I ever hear it sounded in the churches as I was growing up.

The contradictions between the simple and self-justifying world view of my childhood in the church and a growing awareness of the world and its atrocities caused havoc through my teen-age years. The cracks became cleavages as the harsh facts of racism painfully penetrated my consciousness in my youth in Detroit. I felt shocked, betrayed, angry, and painfully implicated in the brutal realities of white racism. My first idealistic impulses drove me to take my concerns to the church with the hope that it would respond. But its defensive reaction and opposition only spawned greater awareness and more action which spawned more reaction . . . it's a familiar story. The church people didn't care to do anything but justify themselves and the country they loved, the country that seemed uglier and uglier to me. As time went on, my family and friends became afraid and confused by my growing alienation from the church.

Feeling lost at that point, I left church, family, and friends and joined the other side. I found my home among those who were also alienated and were seeking to bring about fundamental social change while searching out countercultural alternatives for their own lives. Much study, experience with the unresponsiveness of political, economic, and educational institutions, and the lessons learned from official repression and police violence turned me from an idealistic social crusader to a more sober, more politically wise and radical activist and political organizer.

After a number of years, the weakness and frustrations of the movement, the course of events, and a deep personal and intellectual searching led me to more study, more reflection, and back to the New Testament. As I tried to read the biblical narratives with fresh eyes, I began to see the wholeness and dynamic power of the gospel for the first time, even in the midst of a church whose witness and life-style served to hide and contradict the power of that gospel. My commitment was made to the radical Christ of the New Testament accounts, and I went to seminary only to discover that the church was still responding in much the same way as before. But this time I was more prepared and knew that the biblical faith overturned established religion and was capable of transforming the life of the churches. It seemed a time for the church to rediscover its biblical identity, and, along with others, I began to speak to that issue.

Many are coming to realize something that is at the very heart of Christian faith: The gospel is a message of change; we are continually in need of being transformed; and a biblical faith can never be used to justify complacency in our own lives or in our relationship to society. The church is that collection of people who have come together around the common realization that they are broken persons who need to have their lives changed. That realization should never breed complacency and self-justification. We are of all people those who can admit that we have been wrong, who can scrap old ideas and attitudes when we see their inconsistency. We have all been wrong about so many things, and that's why we need to be remade and renewed in the image of Jesus Christ. When we see that and confess our dependence on God's Spirit, we are freed from the effort to justify ourselves and to be afraid of change.

The church and the world are in great need of a people with the simple intention to faithfully demonstrate a biblical witness in the context of brokenness and suffering, hatred and injustice, violence and oppression.

This book is, more than anything else, a sort of tract. It deals with the Bible and biblical issues throughout, but it is not an exegetical work. Its concerns are deeply theological, but it is not a systematic theology. Issues of politics, economics, and social theory are extensively treated, but it is not a treatise on any of these. It is contemporary to the times but takes up questions that have always and, perhaps, will always be of concern to the life of the church in the world.

Agenda for Biblical People derives not only from a personal pilgrimage but also from the lives of people who, in our own community in Washington, D.C., are learning to share a common life. Common commitments, struggles, and discernment have shaped the book throughout. Also reflected is the experience and insight of the much wider community of those who have been involved with us in a variety of ways, either with our own community or in the growth and development of our monthly publication, the *Post-American*.

The acknowledgements for the book are many: to the people of my community for their love and support; to Joe Roos, Bob Sabath, and Ed Spivey for hours of proofreading, editing, manuscript preparation, and many suggestions; to close friends like Wes Michaelson, John Alexander, and Sharon Gallagher with whom I have shared a common pilgrimage; to the many who have contributed ideas, criticisms, and so much of themselves to our work with the *Post-American*; to the prophetic voices in the church who have called us back to our biblical responsibilities and have been to me examples, teachers, and some of them friends—Jacques Ellul, William Stringfellow, John Howard Yoder, Thomas Merton, Dorothy Day, Clarence Jordan, Will Campbell, Dietrich Bonhoeffer, and a host of others; and to Phyllis Wallis, my mother, who typed the manuscript and has so often shown me the Christian mark of sacrificial love.

AGENDA FOR BIBLICAL PEOPLE

Introduction: Establishment Christianity or Biblical Faith

The old ecclesiastical and doctrinal disputes that have divided the church for so long no longer hold center stage. In fact, many people are openly questioning the importance and even the integrity of the issues that have generated such controversy.

As would be expected in such a climate of change, old categories, labels, and groupings are breaking down. Christians who find themselves returning to their biblical roots are establishing new relationships across confessional and traditional lines. The most important distinctions in theology are no longer between high church and low church, evangelicals and ecumenicals, Protestants and Catholics, Calvinists and Arminians, or whatever else.

What matters most today is whether one is a supporter of establishment Christianity or a practitioner of biblical faith.

Establishment Christianity has made its peace with the established order. It no longer feels itself to be in conflict with the pretensions of the state, with the designs of economic and political power, or with the values and style of life enshrined in the national culture. Establishment Christianity is a religion of accommodation and conformity, which values realism and success more than faithfulness and obedience. It is heavily invested in the political order, the social consensus, and the ideology of the economic system. Its leaders are more comfortable as chaplains than as prophets; its proclamation has been rendered harmless and inoffensive to the wealthy and powerful; and its churchly life has become a mere ecclesiastical reproduction of the values and assumptions of the surrounding environment.

As Christianity has tried to become more respectable and relevant to the culture, it has often lost its adversary relationship to the world. The principle of "separateness from the world" has manifested itself in the mouthing of petty moralisms, while the church has thoroughly accommodated itself to the American way of life and its doctrines of economic and political self-interest, its dogmas of racism and sexism, its commercial and military aggressions. As the major institutions and leaders of establishment Christianity have risen to positions of wealth, prestige, and power, old distinctions have blurred. For example, both conservative evangelicalism and liberal Protestantism have become expressions of establishment Christianity.

The greatest temptation of the people of God has always been to worship other gods and therefore to disobey the first commandment by putting their trust in finite realities rather than in God alone. Unmasking idolatry and turning back to God is a continual task. In our day we must resist the church's servitude to the contemporary idolatries of American life and society, to name a few: the consumptive mentality; the will to power and domination; the oppressions of race, sex, and class; the arrogance of national destiny; and the efficacy of violence. In so doing, we can liberate ourselves from the tyranny of false gods and be free to serve others in God's name.

The concept of "worldliness" must be freed from its strictly private connotation and reapplied to describe the church's false trust in the goodness of the world's powers and institutions, which is conformity to idolatry. Given the strong biblical teaching concerning the fallen condition of the world, it is remarkable how easily the church has become cozy and comfortable with the powers of the world. The church's easy talk about cooperating with, using, and even dominating those powers comes from a biblical naïveté in underestimating the power of the enemy and ends up with the church itself being dominated by the powers of the world. The biblical witness does not support the notion that God's people are meant to be allies of the world's power; rather they are to be a new and different gathering of people whose presence is to play a decisive role in God's action in history. Biblical faith then is quite uncivil.

That God is on the side of the poor and that the Scriptures are uncompromising in their demand for economic and social justice is much more clear biblically than most of the issues over which churches have divided. The Scriptures claim that to know God is to do justice and to plead the cause of the oppressed. Yet this central biblical imperative is one of the first to be purged from a church that has conformed and made accommodations to the established order.

The biblical narratives speak clearly about the structural realities of oppression and the systematized relegating of "the other" to a subhuman status. Using "the other," the despised race or class or sex, is a unique sort of sin and is an issue at the heart of the gospel. Biblical people are called to view systems, societies, cultures, and institutions from the point of view of their victims. This gives the Christian community a unique, perpetually revolutionary role in history.

In Jesus Christ, God takes the form of "the other" as a member of an oppressed race, an exploited class, and a colonized nation. God, in Jesus Christ, becomes poor and oppressed. The paradox and scandal of the incarnation is that God takes the form of a servant and makes himself one with "the others." The church visioned in the New Testament also makes itself one with the poor and the oppressed and assumes the mantle of servanthood after the manner of God in Jesus Christ.

All of this is the witness of Scripture. However, we have suppressed the Bible. We have reduced it to an item on our doctrinal statements, dismissed it as apolitical, and relegated it to a private sphere of holy neutrality in relation to social turmoil and conflict. To do so is fundamentally to misunderstand the meaning of the Word of God which continually breaks into history to judge and transform the human situation. A proper understanding of the biblical witness in human affairs has deep political consequences.

While salvation cannot be earned, the crucial test of its presence in the world is faithful obedience to the will and Word of God. The biblical witness is to God's self-revelation and the saga of the people of God in history. The biblical witness is testimony to the Word of God and discloses the authentic will of God for human life and society. The genuine test of our fidelity to biblical authority is not determined merely by doctrinal affirmations and credal formulations but by whether or not our lives are rooted in the Word of God. Thus, Christian radicalism does not come in turning from the Bible but springs from the deep desire to hear and respond to the Word of God without reservation. Political and social realities must be comprehended and interpreted biblically, and the political character of the biblical witness must be rediscovered.

We are witnessing a growing return to biblical faith. It is a faith that is tested less by a concise doctrine of Scripture than by a life that grows out of the biblical witness. It affirms that one's life rather than one's doctrine is the best test of faithfulness to Scripture. On that score established Christianity has been tested and found wanting.

We are just emerging from a period of biblical illiteracy, neglect, and infidelity. If the church has been irrelevant, we should not blame the Bible. It is only that the biblical witness has been forgotten, ignored, and abused. As Christians, it is our responsibility to bring that witness to light and again recover the powerful potential of a living, biblical faith. In that process, biblical themes begin to take on a fresh meaning and can speak to us with new power and authority.

Central to the renewal of biblical faith is the growing realization among many that the core issue is the urgent priority of rebuilding the church itself and nothing less. The church, as conceived in the New Testament, is commissioned to be a countersign to the world's values and the representative of a new order. The biblical witness sees the new age of the life of the kingdom as existing alongside and in tension with the present age. This is the creative force for change in history, in the biblical sense, in which the life of a covenant people evidences God's activity in judging and liberating. The Bible sees changes as coming about primarily through the presence of the people of God in history, a city on a hill, a demonstration of what human life can be in the love and power of Christ. The new community of God's people exists as an alien force in relation to the old order, and is intended to be an outcropping of the new order—a presentation to the world, and to the very powers of the world, of the possibilities of a new order that is to come and that has already taken root in the life of the world through the death and resurrection of Christ.

It is increasingly clear that any meaningful action in the world on the part of Christians must derive from the experience of the fullness of the body of Christ in the local community of faith. The powerful biblical metaphor that compares the church's life to that of a physical body is now almost completely foreign to most local congregations, which are little more than voluntary associations of autonomous individuals. The basis of prophetic witness and mission in the world is the building of Christian community as a place where our struggles, decisions, and lives can be fully and freely shared. Without that foundation, there is little possibility of Christ being manifest in the fullness and power of which the New Testament speaks. We seek a new and much more biblical evangelistic proclamation with the power to "make disciples." We must understand the building of Christian community as a genuinely revolutionary act which detaches people from the institutional and cultural assumptions that oppress the poor of the earth. For that we need a fresh outpouring of the Holy Spirit to empower us to live transformed lives and to free us from creating new legalisms or seeking to be radically Christian with merely our own human resources.

Biblical people cannot endure the world as it is; they are strangers and pilgrims who seek first the kingdom of God from which comes their motivation and hope. Our communities must demonstrate the "presence of the kingdom" in a confused world and make change and hope visible. Ours is a shared struggle, endeavoring in our priesthood to bring people into an encounter with Christ Jesus and in our prophetic mission challenging the established order of death by the life proclamation of Christ and his kingdom. Corporately, we must commit ourselves to build community, which is the enlivening spirit of our resistance and spiritual growth.

The actions of biblical people are meant to signal the age which is to come, which will make our actions rather uncongenial to the present age. To die on a cross seems utter foolishness to the rulers and the wise of this age, but it was the central act of biblical history in accomplishing God's purposes for human life and society. The scandal of God's servanthood and the foolishness of the cross are meant to be the paradigm for our lives.

Vietnam has become a historical occasion for a renewal of biblical faith. For a whole generation of young Americans, Vietnam has been a central, haunting experience. In a real way, we have grown up on the Vietnam War; it has shattered our illusions, shaped our attitudes, and educated us more profoundly than our classroom studies ever did. Through Vietnam we learned of another America—not of hope, opportunity, and pride, but of arrogance, brutality, and shame. Vietnam has taken us from the patriotism of our childhood through the protest of our adolescence to the resistance of our adulthood. Vietnam was the mirror that revealed to us the truth about our nation, ourselves, and, for some, the meaning of the biblical faith. We will never be the same again.

Many of us can't remember a time when the Vietnam War wasn't being fought. Through five presidential administrations, we watched politicans promise life and bring death. We heard official justifications for the killing and were unconvinced. We learned that our national leaders were liars and perpetrators of genocide. We learned that our protest was "unpatriotic," and, in time, we too rejected the American plan of salvation and began to see the consequences for those who won't conform, for those who stand in the way.

Very few were willing to pay the price of peace as others paid the price of war. Trying to forget all of this is illusive. It is a desire to create still more myths that will save us from facing the harsh facts of reality and will blind us to those very things that resulted in the brutality of Vietnam, things that are still with us and that will continue to cause more destruction if they are not recognized and resisted. We hear cries for reconciliation, but it is a cheap reconciliation which is not based upon the painful judgment of truth and the painful process of repentance. Such is the biblical pattern. Reconciliation is hard and demanding, not to be used as a cover, a way to avoid the truth about ourselves, about our nation, about what we have done. Real healing, lasting healing, will never begin unless those attitudes, values, and institutions that produced Vietnam are exposed and confronted.

The United States government was finally forced out of Indochina. But the departure has not engendered a corresponding change in the commitments, the policies, the attitudes, or the institutional realities that caused Vietnam, that have produced dozens of potential Vietnams around the world, and that will result in ever more exploitation, violence, conflict, and destruction unless these things are changed.

Finally, the Vietnamese have the opportunity to determine their own future. From now on their achievements and failures will be more their own. But what of us? Will we emerge from this exercise in brutality having learned nothing? Can we have perpetrated such suffering and bloodshed and still refuse to examine ourselves and our nation?

Will what we have done to the Vietnamese people change *our* hearts and minds, or will we continue to support the attitudes, values, and institutions that spread the seeds of human misery and conflict? Are we prepared to reap the harvest of injustice and violence again?

Or will we decide to change? Will we decide to live our lives in a different way that might sow the seeds of peace instead of war? Will we withdraw our support from the cause of the rich and powerful and refuse to give our obedience, our sons, our money for their goals and purposes? Will we turn from the politics of death and instead, begin to pursue the politics of life? If we do not, then all the pain and suffering of Vietnam will truly have been in vain.

We are beginning to understand after two centuries what the doctrines of racial and national superiority, of manifest destiny, and of violence have done to the American spirit. The religion of America is still America; and true believers turn their backs on crisis, ignore the consequences for human life, and suspect those who criticize. The machines of war and profit are left unchallenged; technocratic rule remains unaccountable to people as it increasingly threatens human life.

Many of the people and groups who opposed the war do not seem to have either the basis or the motivation, the energy or the capacity, to confront the larger and deeper issues still with us. However, the Vietnam War caused a stirring that could be the greatest source of hope for resistance in the heart of the American corporate state. That stirring is the awakening of a biblical faith within America. This new awareness pleads for change and requires a rethinking of basic assumptions about our society and about ourselves. Our protest must include more than negation and refusal; it must also include affirmation of radical alternatives.

Our affirmation must have an adequate basis for values, vision, and goals which can provide the motivation, direction, and self-criticism necessary in seeking radical change. It must provide a vision that can keep us from the bitterness, despair, hatred, and desperation that causes some to drop out, sell out, or turn their fight for justice and social change into a murderous crusade. We require total transformation, a new understanding of society and ourselves. As the analysis of our dilemma must be radical, so must our solution go to the heart, the root causes of our problems. It must be comprehensive enough to avoid simplistic pitfalls. We must escape the illusion of every simplistic group that looks only beyond itself for the sources of human misery. We must realize that the evil we oppose lies also within ourselves.

The biblical vision provides a vehicle for personal transformation and the emergence of new people who embody the basis for social liberation. To challenge the system, we must be willing to have our own lives changed and become radical ourselves. To repudiate the old is not enough; we must act on the basis of a new reality that we have experienced.

The United States war in Indochina revealed a church captive and morally impotent, a church without a mission. It became clear to many Christians that their churches had become so wedded to the mindset of the American status quo that when the moral crisis of Vietnam emerged the churches had a difficult time making the choice between the cross and the flag.

As a result of Vietnam and the realities of American racism, many Christians have returned to a more biblical theology which generates a critical stance in relationship to the government and the dominant institutions of American power. A central tenet of biblical teaching is that those who have experienced conversion through the gospel are to enter into a life of serious discipleship. In the past, many have understood discipleship in small, private ways that often don't cost very much but not in ways that would make serious demands on a person's life. Many Christians are now learning that obedient discipleship involves a rejection of the greed, the racism, the violence, and the aggressive nationalism that have come to characterize the life of the nation and its institutions. These lessons are being learned at a time when those movements for change present in the sixties have greatly suffered from cooptation and internal weakness. Those movements were unable to generate lasting spiritual resources and provide alternative vision which are, perhaps, the greatest contributions that an awakened Christian conscience could make.

New movements toward costly discipleship and social justice have been occurring among Christians which directly challenge the credibility of those religious leaders who still serve as chaplains to the status quo. With the decline of both the new left and religious liberalism, it is highly possible that the strongest and most sustained thrusts toward social justice may come from those whose faith is Christ centered and who are grounded in an unapologetic biblical faith. Christians must no longer tolerate such a broad credibility gap between doctrinal profession and ethical practice.

They must put their beliefs into practice and demonstrate the power of their theology by the style of life and action it creates in them.

A new evangelical spirit is most characterized by a return to biblical faith and the desire to apply fresh biblical insights to the need for new forms of sociopolitical engagement. In fact, one could argue that these believers take Scripture more seriously than those who accept the Bible doctrinally but balk at the more exacting biblical demands in relation to social justice and Christian lifestyle. While this new spirit is very critical of the conservative religious establishment for its lack of social conscience and ethical compromises, it is no less critical of religious liberalism for its lack of biblical rootage, its disregard for evangelism, and its lack of spiritual life and resources. One hopes that the proclamation and demonstration of a more holistic gospel which is addressed to all that binds and oppresses people, spiritually and economically, personally and politically, could spark renewal and reconciliation among both religious conservatives and religious liberals.

The Vietnam War has taught many the meaning of Christian faith and the cost of our discipleship. It has shown us the need for a biblical faith that goes beyond the bankruptcy of liberal assumptions. It has taught us the need for wholeness in our understanding of the gospel. It has demonstrated the need for radical change in ourselves and in the church and has shown the demand for both personal and social change to be at the heart of the gospel. We have seen the need for a real Christ active in people's lives and present in the life of the world. A new biblical radicalism can provide the basis for people willing to have their own lives changed, to challenge the system, to provide alternative vision.

We are witnessing the growth of a new generation of Christians that has come of age and is making itself heard. A loosely connected, crossconfessional consciousness is finding basic contradictions between the demands of discipleship and the assumptions of American wealth and power. The growing awareness poses a direct challenge to the comfortable relationship of the church with the political and economic status quo. The traditional American civil religion, which blesses the social order rather than calling it into question, is now under serious attack. From many quarters, this civil religion is being named for what it is—misplaced allegiance which usually degenerates into outright idolatry.

It is a narrow orthodoxy that speaks of salvation but is disobedient to the clear teachings of Scripture that faith divorced from an active commitment to social justice is a mockery. It is an empty message that neglects the need of individual transformation and redirection, is easily intimidated by secular assumptions, and balks at the historic confession, "Jesus is Lord." Conservative or liberal, the Christian witness in the nation has been hollow and incomplete, captive to the forces of wealth and power.

Many have come to a Christian commitment in the midst of antiwar and civil rights struggles. Others came to an awareness of the demands of their earlier faith commitments which caused them to feel alienated from the established churches.

Most are simply seeking to rediscover the meaning of the gospel for their lives and their times. Driven to a new understanding of themselves, their nation, and their biblical identity, many are coming to believe that the gospel is a radical premise in its demand and capacity for personal transformation, in its social ethic that drives toward justice, peace, and community, and in its spiritual power that generates belief. The call to discipleship, the call to follow Jesus Christ, demands a fundamental break with the dominant values and conformist patterns of the majority culture.

People are seeking to recover the earliest commitments of Christianity, its historic basis, its radical ethical spirit, and its consciousness of the kingdom of God. Many are coming to understand that the entrance of Jesus Christ into history is nothing less than the inbreaking of a new order on which we are to base our lives.

This process of radicalization does not require the creation of a new theology or value system. It involves rather a return to biblical Christianity. However strong the opposition to the established order, however revolutionary the vision, the basic values and commitments are familiar to those acquainted with the biblical and historic traditions of the church. The startling thing about the insurgents is their affirmation of biblical faith, their sense of continuity with the radical Christian heritage of times past.

The need for a disloyal opposition is greater than ever. It is my contention that the strongest source of such opposition could well spring from awakened biblical conscience in this country. We need a confessing church—a body of people who confess Jesus as Lord and who are prepared to live by their confession. Christians must begin to understand that lives lived under the lordship of Jesus Christ at this point in our history will *necessarily* put us at odds with the leading assumptions of the cultural mainstream, the dominant institutions of political and economic power, and the paralyzing conformity of our church.

What we need most are not national organizations and shrewd strategies to action but a body of people who seek to honor the claims of their discipleship—those who live in active obedience to the call not to conform to this world but to be transformed by the renewing of their minds.

A church seeking to be a sign of Christ's presence in the world is thus a countersign to the values and assumptions of American society and power. Such a witness seeks to call the church out from its American captivity.

This growing body of Christian people, built on the wreckage of the American Dream, will not soon forget the lessons of Vietnam and what it taught us about our nation, ourselves, our faith. We will never be the same again.

1. Gospel of a New Order

Breaking the Cycle

With us therefore worldly standards have ceased to count in our estimate of any man; . . . When anyone is united to Christ, there is a whole new world; the old order has gone, and a new order has already begun.

From first to last this has been a work of God. He has reconciled us men to himself through Christ, and he has enlisted us in this service of reconciliation. What I mean is, that God was in Christ reconciling the world to himself, no longer holding men's misdeeds against them, and that he has entrusted us with the message of reconciliation. We come therefore as Christ's ambassadors. It is as if God were appealing to you through us: in Christ's name, we implore you, be reconciled to God! (2 Cor. 5:16–21, NEB).

As I was growing up in Middle America, certain things about the nature and structure of the world I knew began to make a deep impression. Becoming involved in the radical student movement, the antiwar struggle, and the movements of the black and poor served to deepen my impressions. During those years, the most powerful fact of reality that continued to confront me was something I would now call the cycle of the world. Beyond the visible devils of racism, poverty, and war, there seemed to be a cycle operating in the world which was inherent in the very structure of things. The world appeared to be dominated by a whole cycle of

13

injustice and violence, of exploitation and manipulation, of profit and power, of self-interest and competition, of hate and fear, of loneliness and brokenness, a cycle whose final meaning seemed to be death itself. This moral cycle of death appeared to be pervasive and seemed to be at the root of the condition of the world.

Like many others, I became involved in social and political movements which were fighting against that cycle of oppression, human suffering, and moral death. However, we were never really able to break that cycle. Mostly, we were only able to protest its existence. In fact, our very lives and, I think, the life of most of our movements came to reflect that cycle and, ultimately, was co-opted by it. Certainly, the major social movements of recent American history have been without adequate foundations to sustain themselves.

The thing that struck me so powerfully about the claim and meaning of the gospel was that, in Jesus Christ, the cycle of death in the world had been broken. The gospel presented in the New Testament is a scandal to the values and standards of the world whose condition is dominated by the cycle of death. While assimilation, complicity, and compromise best describe the modern church's relationship to the world, the gospel is in direct collision with the world system. Talk of realism, respectability, and reasonableness dominates the conversations of contemporary religion, but the New Testament speaks of the abandonment, insecurity, persecution, and exile that come from seeking *first* the kingdom. A church of comfort, property, privilege, and position stands in sharp contrast with the biblical description of the people of God as aliens, exiles, sojourners, strangers, and pilgrims. "If the world hates you, it hated me first, as you know well. If you belonged to the world, the world would love its own; but because you do not belong to the world, because I have chosen you out of the world, for that reason the world hates you" (John 15:18, 19, NEB).

The claim of the New Testament writers is that the power of the cycle of the world that holds men, women, and institutions so captive has been decisively broken by the cross and resurrection of Jesus Christ. The absolute authority and dominion of the destructive forces and structures of the world has been ended by the inauguration of a whole new order in human affairs called the kingdom of God, according to the New Testament evangelists. The gospel calls for radical allegiance to a kingdom that is at fundamental variance with the "principalities and powers" which rule the world system. The standards and values of the world undergo a transvaluation, a reversal, an inversion in Jesus Christ. A commitment to Christ entails a radical change in our relationship to money and possessions, violence and war, power, status, success, leadership, ideology, and the state. Our relationship to Christ gives us a new relationship to persons and especially to the poor, the weak, the broken, the outcasts, the "enemies," and the victims of the various systems of the world. In his Nazareth inaugural, Jesus speaks of those who are so central to the meaning of his coming:

> The Spirit of the Lord is upon me,
> Because he anointed me to preach the gospel to the poor.
> He has sent me to proclaim release to the captives,
> And recovery of sight to the blind,
> To set free those who are downtrodden,
> To proclaim the favorable year of the Lord
>   (Luke 4:18, 19, NASB)

In this kingdom, whoever would save his life will lose it, the last are first and the first are last, and whoever would be great must become the servant of all which is the principle sign of the kingdom.

The proclamation of the New Testament is the gospel of the kingdom, a gospel of a "new order," a "new creation," a "new world," a "new age," as it is variously referred to by the biblical writers. Jesus proclaims that a new age has come and calls us to be free of former allegiances, attachments, securities, and assumptions in the present age, to break from our bondage to the standards of the world that are passing away. Clearly, the New Testament evangel is something much more than a gospel of individual salvation and personal fulfillment. The evangel is something much more than a gospel of social action. It is even more than an attempted synthesis which combines a personal gospel with social reform. In fact, the meaning of the gospel that dominates the New Testament is not usually the same as the meaning of the various gospels that dominate the evangelism and preaching of our churches. The gospel of the kingdom is the central message of the New Testament. The inauguration of a whole new order in Jesus Christ and the establishing of a new peoplehood whose common life bears witness to that new order in history is what the New Testament message seems to be all about. The proclamation is not a personal gospel, not a social gospel, not even a gospel of "both," but rather the gospel of a new order and a new people. The evangel is not merely a set of principles, ethics, and moral teachings. It is about a Person and the meaning of his coming.

The first evangelists preached the gospel as God's "good news" in Jesus Christ who brings reconciliation and a new creation, who has "dethroned" and "disarmed" the "powers" of the world that have previously held absolute sway in people's lives, who has established a "new humanity," a radically new kind of community empowered by the Holy Spirit to live in obedience to Christ in contradiction to the standards of the world. Therefore, for the followers of Christ, life is not to perpetuate the cycle of the world. The Christian community must demonstrate that the cycle of death in the world can be broken, indeed, that it has *already* been broken in Jesus Christ. The apostle Paul described our former condition as being "dead in your trespasses and sins, in which you once walked, according to the course of this world, according to the prince of the power of the air." But now, says Paul, God has "made us alive together with Christ," has "united us to him" in his death and resurrection, and has raised Christ from the dead so "we too might walk in newness of life" (Eph. 2 and Rom. 5).

The New Testament sees the Christian community as the place where, first of all in its own shared common life, the cycle of the world begins to be broken. By rendering impotent the power of those things which oppress and divide people, the facts of race, class, and sex, the Christian community demonstrates the victory of Christ who has "broken down the walls" and "put to death the enmity" between people (Eph. 2).

There is neither Jew nor Greek, there is neither slave nor freeman, there is neither male nor female; for you are all one in Christ Jesus (Gal. 3:28, NASB).

By showing the irrelevance of the oppressive and divisive factors of the world, the Christian community begins to be witness to the breaking of the cycle of death. By the quality of their new style of life, by their active presence in the world, the Christian community can show that the cycle of death in the world need no longer have dominion over us, that new possibilities of human life and society emerge as we give our lives over to Christ and his kingdom.

The possibility of breaking the cycle of death in the world and ending its dominion in people's lives is something I did not see in the other ideological and philosophical options in my experience. However, the victory of Christ must be concretely demonstrated by the Christian community in history. A church that is merely perpetuating the cycle of death in the world and is a mere reflection of it has lost its identity. A church that is living in support of the cycle of the world system is disobedient and fails to comprehend the meaning of the death and resurrection of Christ. When the church takes its values and standards from its culture and society, when it takes its authority from Caesar and the various powers of the world, the victory of Christ is blasphemed because the life of the church has become conformed to the very things for which Christ was crucified. A church whose life is lived in complicity and conformity to the world and its cycle of death again nails Jesus Christ to the cross.

Our most persistent problem is that we try to make the claims of Christ negotiable with the claims and demands of the world. The New Testament seems to say rather clearly that, for those who would be disciples, the claims of Christ are nonnegotiable. The principal way the world system seeks to overcome the church is by trying to squeeze the church into its own mold, to reduce the church to conformity. Therefore, the church must resist the constant temptation to reduce the claims of Christ, soften the demands of the gospel, ease the tension between the church and the world, and allow the ever radical message to be squeezed into more comfortable and congenial forms and styles. If we truly believe that Jesus Christ has broken the authority and dominion of the corporate and personal powers of death in the world, then the life of the church in the world must demonstrate some signs and indications of that victory. The community of believers must expect to find themselves at variance with the social consensus, the political conformity, and the popular wisdom of their society, for they are witnesses to a whole new order.

No condemnation now hangs over the head of those who are "in Jesus Christ." For the new spiritual principle of life "in" Christ lifts me out of the old vicious circle of sin and death (Rom. 8:1, 2, Phillips).

The Call to Repentance

Repent; for the kingdom of heaven is at hand (Matt. 4:17, NASB).

The coming of Christ always brings with it the call to repentance and radical change. The social and political upheaval caused by the entrance of Christ into history is seen from the outset when Mary proclaimed a hymn of praise upon receiving the word that she would bear the Son of God.

He has shown strength with his arm, he has scattered the proud in the imagination of their hearts, he has put down the mighty from their thrones, and exalted those of low degree; he has filled the hungry with good things, and the rich he has sent empty away (Luke 1:51–53, RSV).

Even as a small baby, Christ was rightly viewed as a political threat to the established authorities. Matthew described how King Herod, fearing a competing claim to his power and authority, ordered the massacre of the innocents, forcing Jesus and his parents to flee from the land. Political persecution was also the fate of John the Baptist whose ministry of preparing the way for Christ called people to repentance and redirection in their personal and corporate lives. All this was in the tradition of the Old Testament prophets who boldly proclaimed the judgment of God upon the injustice of the social order and the sins of the people and called all those who would hear to repentance and a better way.

A call to repentance would sound rather foolish and scandalous in our sophisticated technological societies that seem to have lost any capacity for self-examination or for fundamental redirection. The biblical narratives suggest that people and nations living in the midst of sin will often fail to recognize the true nature of their condition. The capacity for repentance is swallowed up by personal and national self-righteousness and pride. Personal accountability is lost in a sea of social conformity and in the driving ambition to succeed in a game whose rules have been carefully laid down. Responsibility for human atrocity and moral brutality is evaded by the disclaimer of "just following orders" or by appealing to the demands of political realism and economic necessity.

Examination of conscience is a difficult task. We want to look everywhere but to ourselves for the sources of our problems and the problems of others. Nations, individuals, and even the church resist self-examination and fundamental change. But is this not the very meaning of the gospel? We are exposed for who we are, confronted by the claims of a sovereign Lord, and called to complete redirection.

The way of Jesus was to call people to repentance and discipleship. That call was at the center of his ministry, and it must be at the center of ours. Calling peoples to repentance and redirection has profound political meaning, and, until we "politicized" Christians recognize that, our politics will be terribly inadequate.

The Greek word for repentance is *metanoia*, which literally means to change the form, to turn the mind around, to take on a whole new identity. It means a transformation of life that is more basic, deeper, and more far-reaching than our common understanding of the word *repentance*. Our understanding of the word *repentance* carries a sense of guilt and being sorry for something.

In sharp contrast, the Greek word *metanoia* speaks the language of transformation, meaning a change of orientation, character, and direction that is so pronounced and dramatic that the very form and purpose of a life is decisively altered, reshaped, and turned around. Clarence Jordan, in describing the meaning of the word *metanoia*, likens it to the metamorphosis of a moth being made over into a beautiful butterfly. The analogy is a good one, for the words *metanoia* and *metamorphosis* have the same root.

Jesus used this powerful word *metanoia* in describing the kind of change that must be undergone before one is prepared to enter into the kingdom of God. This language of change is so strong and demanding because the coming of Christ heralds a new age, the coming of a new order in human affairs. Matthew quotes Isaiah's prophecy concerning Christ: "The people who were sitting in darkness saw a great light, and to those who were sitting in the land and shadow of death, upon them a light dawned." Then the apostle records, "From that time Jesus began to preach and say, 'Repent [or *metanoia*]; for the kingdom of heaven is at hand'" (Matt. 4:16, 17, NASB). Jesus is here saying that we must be equipped and prepared for participation in a new order that has come to transform the world. He calls us to change our whole way of thinking and living, for the kingdom is impinging upon us.

Now the one depends upon the other. You can't talk about the need for personal transformation apart from the coming of the kingdom of God. To do so is to reduce the gospel to a completely private affair, to some sort of metaphysical transaction that "saves" individuals but is unrelated to history and the rest of humanity. Conversely, you can't speak of the kingdom apart from the necessity of persons repenting of sin, turning to Christ, and having their lives radically transformed. To do that is to have a secular vision of the kingdom as some kind of utopian dream that can be built with good intentions and human hands. The message of Jesus, at the outset of his ministry, is that we must undergo radical change and be given a whole new identity, precisely *because* the new order of the kingdom of God is upon us.

The inbreaking of the kingdom of God into history confronts us

with a new order so different from the present condition of the
world and of our lives that the change required to enter into it is
described by Jesus as a "new birth." "Truly, truly, I say to you,
unless one is born again, he cannot see the kingdom of God"
(John 3:3, NASB). The whole New Testament witnesses to the
good news that the light of Christ has come into the world enabling us to be taken out of the darkness and placed into a whole
new order of things. The call to repentance means that we must
turn from our former ways and, in Christ, be changed, equipped,
and enabled to participate in the new order that has come to
replace the old. It involves a new birth, a new life, and a complete
change of ways (1 Pet. 1, 2). Most centrally, the call is to a
change of allegiance, a change of loyalty, a liberation from all
other claims of lordship to the service of Christ. A response to
that call is a placement within the messianic community of those
who experience *metanoia* and whose life and mission is a sign of
the new order.

But we are afraid of that. We want to stay in the old order
while we sing the praises of the new. We are not satisfied with the
old order but still have most of our securities there. "For where
your treasure is, there will your heart be also" (Matt. 6:21,
NASB). While professing loyalty to the kingdom, we are assimilated
by the culture and subservient to the religion of the nation-state.
Unable to choose between Caesar and Christ, we patronize both.
We preach about the new order but are hesitant to invest our lives
in it. "So because you are lukewarm, and neither hot nor cold, I
will spit you out of My mouth. . . . Those whom I love, I reprove
and discipline; be zealous therefore, and repent" (Rev. 3:16, 19,
NASB).

The witness of Scripture is clear that there is no salvation without repentance. Conversion without repentance is foreign to the
gospel. The New Testament speaks of repentance as something
that needs to be demonstrated. Those who repented and turned to
Christ were to "bring forth fruits worthy of repentance" (Matt.
3:8 and Acts 26:20). Repentance means a radical break with the
past and a determination to follow the path of obedience to Christ.

The New Testament evangel demanded a response. Men and women were challenged to decide for or against the God who had decided for them in Jesus Christ. Repentance from personal and corporate sin, from the former way of life in servitude to the powers of the world, from every other lordship than that of Jesus Christ were all involved. Repentance brought more than an emotional release; it brought a new life-style of obedient faith and active participation in the community of faith whose common life was characterized by the twin features of forgiveness and liberation in Christ.

The proclamation of the gospel today must provide a meaningful call to repentance. The New Testament call to repentance was sounded in a situation of political oppression and revolutionary upheaval, of human suffering and spiritual blindness. The call to repentance today cannot be meaningful in a social and political vacuum. Rather, it must be addressed to the concrete situation of our society. Where violence and force have become the means to all ends, the call to repentance must proclaim the gospel that came "to guide our feet into the way of peace" (Luke 1:79, NASB). Where the facts of race, class, and sex are used to oppress and divide, the gospel message must speak of the meaning of the cross and resurrection of Christ in abolishing former divisions and barriers and creating a new humanity where all men and women are reconciled as one. When the wealth of the affluent imprisons so many in poverty and the rich nations and classes worship the god of mammon while the poor starve, the gospel must be preached as a social and economic revolution and the church called to be the servant of the poor. In a political environment where power is its own justification and where manipulation and self-perpetuation are the dominant style of leadership, the evangel must testify to a messiah who "did not come to be served, but to serve, and to give His life a ransom for many" (Matt. 20:28, NASB). The preaching of the gospel in our times, as in other times, must involve the call to "Repent, for the kingdom of heaven is at hand."

Making Disciples

All authority has been given to Me in heaven and on earth. Go therefore and make disciples of all the nations, baptizing them in the name of the Father and the Son and the Holy Spirit, teaching them to observe all that I commanded you; and lo, I am with you always, even to the end of the age (Matt. 28:18–20, NASB).

This great commission, recorded at the end of the Book of Matthew, gives Christ's followers the instruction to go and "make disciples" of all peoples, "teaching them to observe" *all* that Christ had commanded and taught them. They go in the name of Jesus Christ who has been given all authority, who has overcome the world and the militant cycle of death itself, who has inaugurated a whole new order in human affairs called the kingdom of God, who has called out a faithful people to serve as active agents of that kingdom which he will himself consummate at the end of the age.

The great tragedy of modern evangelism is in calling many to belief but few to obedience. The failure has come in separating belief from obedience, which renders the gospel message confusing and strips the evangelistic proclamation of its power and authority. The evangelistic question has become what do we believe *about* Christ rather than are we willing to forsake all and follow him. When the theology of faith is torn apart from the life of faith, what results is an evangelism that has more to do with doctrine than with transformation. In our times, obedience to Christ has been seriously compromised by an evangelism of easy belief and simple formulas. The radical demands of Christ have been reduced and all but obliterated by the modern evangelism that takes the liberty to conceal the cost of discipleship. Most of our contemporary Christian proclamations, regardless of labels and theological distinctions, are not involved in the making of disciples and are, therefore, failing to respond to the commission of Christ to his church. In fact, a clear proclamation of the gospel with the demonstrated power to "make disciples" is precisely what is most lacking in the churches. In the midst of theological cleavage and doctrinal disputes, one is hard pressed to know where to turn for the kind of evangelism with the courage to take Christ at his word by teaching men and women all that he commanded. Instead, that which offends, that which would necessitate fundamental change, that which would disrupt the social order, that which would threaten the power and policies of the state, that which challenges the needs and character of the economic system, or that which undercuts the vested interests of the established church, is all carefully removed from the evangelistic proclamation. The consequence of this radical surgery is *evangelism without the gospel.*

This evangelism of conformity provides no challenge to the dominant social, economic, and political values of a society but, rather, operates within the framework and consensus of those values. Therefore, such evangelism enjoys the blessing of the state and even the respect of the popular culture. Restricting its message to personal morality and private salvation, the church becomes friend and spiritual advisor to the rich and powerful, an honored chaplain who identifies with the purposes and destiny of the nation. There is a long and tragic history of political rulers supporting religious concern which can serve their interests while suppressing religious conviction which threatens their regime. The former is blessed, its leaders are used, its activities endorsed, while the latter is put down for "meddling in political affairs." The state will often give "religious freedom" to church leaders and evangelists who are willing to allow the gospel to be stripped of its political meaning and to preach an individualistic message which is no threat to injustice and oppression and is prophetically impotent. Such evangelism is biblically irresponsible and implicitly endorses a low view of Christ by suggesting the gospel is not relevant to the wider issues of human life and society.

The commission to make disciples is violated in different ways. It is violated by a secular theology that doesn't recognize the need for a real Christ, actively transforming people's lives. The commission is also violated by a doctrinally proper theology that presumes the mere proclamation of the grace of God available in Jesus Christ to be the same thing as making disciples. We are

faced, on the one hand, with those who have dropped the proclamation of the gospel altogether and, on the other hand, with
those who have substituted a truncated evangelism for the preaching of the good news of the gospel of the kindgom.

While most churches speak of the grace of God, the New Testament demand for absolute obedience and unconditional discipleship is often missing. Dietrich Bonhoeffer's warning against
"cheap grace" without the cost of discipleship, given many years
ago in another crisis situation, needs to be raised again today. Too
often, our preaching has become frozen into cultural or ideological
molds, and the people perish without a biblical vision of the gospel or a visible demonstration of its transforming power. Our most
critical need is for a proclamation of the gospel in word and deed
with the power to break free from conformist patterns, vested
interests, and ideological necessities so that the living Christ might
liberate and remake us, transforming our hearts and minds and
lives.

Most simply put, we are contending today for a proclamation
and demonstration of the gospel with the power to make disciples.
We must resist a spiritualized or privatized message which does
not issue forth in radical obedience to all that Christ commanded,
and we must resist the secularization of the gospel in a way that
denies its spiritual power. We must contend against the constant
temptation to accommodate the gospel message to the world in a
captive civil religion that doesn't threaten the social and political
order. We are contending, instead, for a living affirmation of the
lordship of Jesus Christ which brings his message of life, liberation, healing, wholeness, justice, and reconciliation into active
confrontation and combat with the pervasive power of oppression,
sin, and death of this present age.

Our gospel is God's good news of Jesus Christ as Savior and
Lord who brings forgiveness, reconciliation, and a new creation;
of his cross and resurrection which have won and sealed the victory over the forces of destruction and death; and of a radically
new kind of community, a new humanity united in Christ and
empowered by the Holy Spirit to live according to the standard

and character of a new order. Thus, the coming of Christ heralds a new age, a new birth, a new peoplehood. The evangelistic proclamation of the church must make all this clear and visible. This is the message that must take concrete shape and form in history if the gospel is to have any incarnational reality. The personal, social, political, economic, global, and cosmic meaning of the gospel must be recovered and clearly set forth if we wish to restore integrity to the church's evangelism.

> I can only tell you what I believe. I believe
>   I cannot be saved by foreign policies
>   I cannot be saved by sexual revolutions
>   I cannot be saved by the gross national product
>   I cannot be saved by nuclear deterrents
>   I cannot be saved by aldermen, priests, artists, plumbers,
>   city planners, social engineers,
>   nor by the Vatican, nor by the World Buddhist Association
>   nor by Hitler nor by Joan of Arc
>   nor by angels and archangels nor by powers and dominations
>   I can be saved only by Jesus Christ.
>   *Daniel Berrigan*

The salvation Christ brings is the gift which frees men and women from all that binds and oppresses them and enables them to "walk in newness of life." Emancipated by Christ, persons are freed from the alienation of their own lives, the yoke of self-interest, the idolatries of the social and political order, the oppressive rule of the principalities and powers, the claims of imperial states, and the moral authority of death. Faith is the acceptance and celebration of that gift of life, freely given by the grace of God, in the midst of a world dominated by death. The response of faith always embraces the call to discipleship, the call to show forth the reality of the new life and freedom by following in obedience to Christ. The call to faith and to discipleship are the same and cannot be separated.

Then Jesus told his disciples, "If any man would come after me, let him deny himself and take up his cross and follow me. For whoever would save his life will lose it, and whoever will lose his life for my sake will find it. For what will it profit a man, if he gains the whole world and forfeits his life?" (Matt. 16:24–26, RSV).

The New Testament story of the "rich young ruler" demonstrates that Jesus had only one criterion for salvation: unchallenged, unconditional allegiance. While the exacting demands of discipleship turned the wealthy young man away, "for he had many possessions," he might have found a comfortable and prestigious place in many of today's congregations. Here was a man who was morally upright among his peers, a respected and influential citizen. And yet, Jesus said to him,

If you wish to go the whole way, go, sell your possessions, and give to the poor, and then you will have riches in heaven; and come, follow me (Matt. 19:21, NEB).

After the young man turned away and departed in heavy sorrow, Jesus continued to teach his disciples about the great obstacle of wealth and possessions.

I tell you this: a rich man will find it hard to enter the kingdom of Heaven. I repeat, it is easier for a camel to pass through the eye of a needle than for a rich man to enter the kingdom of God (Matt. 19:23, 24, NEB).

Also striking is the conversion of Zaccheus, a tax collector who had robbed from the poor (Luke 19:1–10). The significance of that conversion story is not that Zaccheus was so short he had to climb a tree to see Jesus, as children are often taught in their Sunday school lesson. The biblical witness to the conversion of Zaccheus shows that his repenting of sin and turning to Jesus involved *making reparations to the poor*. Because we profit from oppressive economic structures and relationships, the affluent countries are nations of rich young rulers and publicans who have robbed the poor. What, then, does the call to repentance and the gospel of the kingdom have to say to us?

Modern evangelism is always concerned with asking how many

have been converted and brought into the churches. It is seldom asked how many have been turned away because of the radical claims Christ is making on their lives. A dangerous respect for numerical success has led to reducing the demands of the gospel, blurring the meaning of discipleship, and accommodating the evangelistic message to what the audience will find more easily acceptable. Rene Padilla, of Argentina, spoke to this point with clarity in his address to the World Congress on Evangelization in Lausanne:

. . . the Gospel of the cross leaves open the possibility for people to re- ject Christ because of finding his claims too costly and admits that there are cases when it is better not to have certain people in the church, even though it means a smaller membership. Was not this Jesus' attitude in dealing with the rich young ruler (Mark 10:17–22) or with the multitudes at the peak of his popularity (Luke 14:25–32)? Furthermore, if a truncated Gospel necessarily results in churches that are themselves a denial of the Gospel, in speaking of the numerical ex- pansion of the church it is not out of place to ask what kind of church is being multiplied. It may be that such a multiplication turns out to be a multiplication of apostasy.

Padilla continues,

The task of the evangelist in communicating the Gospel is not to make it easier, so that people will respond positively, but to make it clear. Neither Jesus nor his apostles ever reduced the demands of the gospel in order to make converts. No cheap grace, but God's kindness which is meant to lead to repentance, provides the only solid basis for disciple- ship. He who accommodates the Gospel to the mood of the day, in order to make it more palatable, does so because he has forgotten the nature of Christian salvation—it is not man's work, but God's.

Faithfulness to Christ requires a faithful proclamation of the radical demands of the gospel. Anything less is a disservice to Christ and to those who would respond without a clear idea of the nature of the commitment called for by the gospel. Cheap conver- sion runs the grave danger of saying yes to the sin, instead of saying yes to the sinner. The grace of God is meant to justify the sinner and never to justify the sin. In Bonhoeffer's prophetic words, "Cheap grace is the deadly enemy of our Church.... Grace is costly because it calls us to follow Jesus Christ. It is costly because it costs a man his life, and it is grace because it gives a man the only true life" (*Cost of Discipleship*, p. 47). The salvation that has cost God so much cannot be offered in cheap conversion.

A central weakness of many contemporary doctrines of salvation is that they produce a sole concern for personal redemption and justification before God apart from any reference to the kingdom of God. The common failing of many evangelistic proclamations comes when there is a concentration upon getting one's heart right with God, which predominates over a primary concern for the meaning and coming of the kingdom. Christ the atoning sacrifice for sins is stressed to the exclusion of Christ the bringer and bearer of a new order in history that is in radical contradiction to the standards and structures of the present world. While the coming of the kingdom takes center stage in the evangelistic proclamations of the New Testament, it is often pushed to the periphery or brushed aside altogether in modern evangelism. Without the central focus of the gospel of the kingdom, the Christian message loses its core and integrating center. When personal transformation and redemption are separated from active participation in the kingdom of God, the evangelistic message easily degenerates into something which supports self-interest and vested interests in a society.

The forgiveness and reconciliation brought about in Christ are integrally connected to a change of allegiance and commitment to the kingdom. Indeed, belief in the redeeming and reconciling work of Christ and obedience to his kingdom form a living unity. The forgiveness of sins and justification through the death and resurrection of Christ are organically related to belief and participation in the coming kingdom. The "saving" of individuals apart from a radical allegiance and living witness to the kingdom of God takes the heart out of the gospel. Conversely, a belief in the kingdom apart from the transformation of persons in Christ and through the power of the Holy Spirit is a false hope that loses the empowering dynamic of the gospel. The work of Christ in the life of an individual supplies the ground and possibility for participation in the new order that has invaded the world in Christ. To be Christian is to be possessed and dominated by the kingdom of God. Salvation must not be seen as merely an individual event but, rather, as a world event in which the individual has a part. The kingdom of God has come to transform the world and us with it by the power of God in Jesus Christ. The cross of Christ is not only the symbol of our atonement but the very pattern and definition of our lives, the very *means* of the new order that has invaded the world in Christ.

I believe that our distorted concepts of salvation are, in large part, due to the pervasive influence of individualism in the churches. The ideologies of individualism are certainly at variance with the biblical understanding of salvation. In Scripture, personal realities are never divorced from social and historical realities. To do so is to invite moral atrocity. The terrible fear of a Vietnamese mother whose family may be exterminated by American bombs becomes translated into a "political" issue that is somehow outside the boundaries of the concerns of proper religion. The oppression and destruction of racial minorities becomes a "social" problem which we can choose to deal with or not. The misery and deprivation of the poor becomes an "economic" matter unrelated to *our* personal consumption, life-style, and involvement in the economic system. We easily forget that "social problems" are very personal realities for those who suffer from them. In other words, the victims of war, racism, and poverty experience the consequences of our social problems in deeply personal ways.

Only a white society can regard racism as merely a social problem. Only the affluent can view poverty simply as an economic question. Only a war-making nation can understand its destructive policies as just a political issue. Biblically, human suffering is a deeply spiritual issue and an urgent moral concern of the people of God regardless of the way the world may label and categorize its various "problems." A relationship to Christ always involves a vital relationship to persons and the conditions of their lives. In Scripture, there is no salvation apart from one's brothers and sisters. All that would bind and oppress, all that would hold people captive and prevent them from being what they were created to be, falls within the range and scope of the concern of biblical faith.

An individualistic understanding of the gospel carries the danger of making salvation into just another commodity that can be consumed for personal fulfillment and self-interest, for a guarantee of happiness, success, moral justification, or whatever else a consumer audience feels it needs. Some evangelistic proclamations go so far as to offer the real possibilities of financial success and blessing, personal advancement, community respectability, a well-balanced personality, social popularity, and the patriotic virtues of good citizenship for those who would be "saved" and get their hearts right with God. Conservative evangelical understandings of the gospel have often produced a private view of the gospel with a distorted emphasis on the consequences of the Christian message on the individual heart or psyche apart from the corporate, social, political, economic, global, and cosmic meaning of the gospel of the kingdom that has invaded the history of the world. Reducing the gospel to only personal and existential terms, the Christian message is easily co-opted by larger social and political forces which seek to make religion an appendage of the established order which assists in the task of furthering socialization, social adjustment, and conformity.

The meaning of evangelism, then, is the proclamation and demonstration of the "good news" that a new order is upon us and calls us to redirection, to change our former ways of thinking and living, to turn to Jesus Christ for a new way of life, to enter into the fellowship of a new community. Our understanding of evangelism will not go very far without a strong and sensitive awareness of the crucial issues of human life and society in our own times. Evangelism can never take place in a vacuum, in isolation from the critical questions and events that shape the context in which the gospel must be lived and proclaimed. The scope of our evangelism must be at least as pervasive as the power of sin itself. As sin and death manifest themselves institutionally, politically, and economically as well as personally, our evangelism must bring the gospel into active confrontation with the personal and corporate character and dimensions of sin and death.

Much contemporary evangelism has become calculating and compassionless as it has become successful in numerical terms. Many evangelists must plead guilty to the charge of holding a low view of Christ in restricting the gospel to the personal, private, and "religious" issues of life. This sort of preaching offers salvation without "making disciples" who live in radical obedience to Christ as active agents of the kingdom of God. Our evangelism, itself, must be converted to a deeper meaning of the gospel and the lordship of Christ. It may well be that the churches themselves must become a target of evangelism, to be awakened continually to the good news of the gospel of the kingdom.

Christian conversion is not static. Rather, we are instructed to "work out our salvation with fear and trembling." We commit ourselves to a continuing reorientation to the will of God and the reconciliation brought about in Jesus Christ. The gospel is of a living Christ who makes "all things new." The criterion to test the integrity of our evangelism is whether our message is as radical as the gospel. Are we softening the demands of Christ and adopting a method to persuade people to "make a decision" rather than clearly demonstrating, in word and deed, the costly character of discipleship? Are we trying to make the gospel respectable and self-fulfilling rather than allowing it to make radical demands upon our lives, to change us in fundamental ways? The quality of conversion lies in its wholeness.

When someone is converted to Christ, he or she does not receive an automatic pass to celestial bliss but is called to take up a cross and follow in obedience the one who fed the hungry, healed the sick, was a friend to all manner of men and women, most identified with the poor, the oppressed, the weak, and broken, blessed the peacemakers, and was executed as a political criminal and subversive. This is the Christ of the New Testament. There is no other. Preaching another Christ, serving another Christ, worshiping another Christ, is paying homage to an idol who is the incarnation of humankind rather than the incarnation of God. It is the Christ of the New Testament that we turn to for life because, like Peter, we have nowhere else to turn.

Evangelism that is obedient to the great commission brings fundamental and costly change in personal, communal, political, and economic values and relationships. It holds the individual and corporate dimensions of the gospel as inseparable. It bears the gospel of the kingdom which pronounces the judgment of God upon the present order of injustice and carries the promise of a new order and a new people. We can no longer talk of people's need for salvation apart from our responsibility to give the kingdom of God a presence in our generation. Therefore, evangelism in our times must begin, not through new methods and techniques, but by repentance on the part of the church. The church must be continually reoriented to the gospel, a community of those freed from the service of self, of nation-states, of ideologies, of systems, of movements, of political realism, of economic necessity, of social conformity—freed for the service of the kingdom of God.

A New Style of Life

Jesus announced the beginning of the new order, preached repentance, and began immediately to call his disciples saying, "Follow me and I will make you fishers of men." The call was to absolute allegiance and obedient faith, and "they immediately left their nets and followed him." As always, former securities and attachments are left behind as the choice is made to follow Christ, as we "find" our life by "losing it" for the sake of the gospel. Then Christ began to go about healing the infirmities of the people, preaching the gospel of the kingdom, and teaching his disciples how the life to be found in the new order of Christ was at odds with the mindset and values of the world.

The apostle James well described the difference between living faith and empty faith. Dead faith bears no fruit, shows no evidence of transformation. The criterion to judge faith is the quality of the believer's life as a living witness to the gospel, not mere assent to doctrine and creed. In the Gospel of Luke, Jesus rebukes those who call him lord but fail to demonstrate obedience: "Why do you call me 'Lord, Lord,' and not do what I tell you?" In Matthew, Jesus again warns those who call his name but go unrecognized because their lives show no fruits of obedience.

Not every one who says to me, "Lord, Lord," shall enter the kingdom of heaven, but he who does the will of my father who is in heaven. On that day many will say to me, "Lord, Lord, did we not prophesy in your name, and cast out demons in your name, and do many mighty works in your name?" And then will I declare to them, "I never knew you; depart from me, you evildoers" (Matt. 7:21–23, RSV).

He goes on to say that anyone who hears his words and does not act upon them is like a foolish man who builds his house on sand.

Verbal and intellectual assent to Christ is not enough; a clear demonstration is demanded. Christ's disciples are not those who have voiced their agreement and registered their support but those who are basing their lives upon his kingdom. Our discipleship is tested throughout our lives by whether we love the things that are in the world and are anxious over the securities that most concern others or whether we "abide in Christ" and seek first the kingdom (1 John 2; Luke 12). Jesus says that his disciples must count the cost before making the choice to follow him (Luke 14:26–35).

The Sermon on the Mount is a manifesto of the kingdom of God and a summary text on the meaning of the beginning of the new order in Jesus Christ. The teachings of the sermon radically conflict with usual and common standards of reason, realism, and responsibility. In fact, it is precisely their unusual and uncommon character that testifies to the uniqueness of the new order begun by Christ. They are not a prescription for a happy and successful life but rather carry the expectation of persecution. They are not rules to be imposed upon a society. The sermon is merely a description of how one lives and acts if one has been transformed by Jesus Christ (*metanoia*). There is the assumption that those who follow Christ and live that way will be a minority in any society. It is also assumed that such a way of living will be a social upheaval in any social or political system. It is evident that this social upheaval will be especially to the advantage of the victims and dispossessed of the various systems of the world. The clear expectation is that living in such a way will be appalling to the common sense of any social system or political order, especially in regard to Christ's teaching concerning money, fame, violence, power, security, the poor, and how we respond to our enemies. It is expected that the established order will respond accordingly. It can be said that the way of living described in the Sermon on the Mount is neither practical nor effective but utterly foolish if God does not love us and Christ is not our Savior and Lord.

The question of the Christian style of life in the world is the crucial point where the truth and power of the gospel will be most severely tested. Theology and doctrine have no power apart from a style of life in the world that is consistent with what is believed. Jacques Ellul, the French social critic and theologian, comments on the priority of creating a new style of life:

In order that Christianity today may have a point of contact with the world, it is less important to have theories about economic and political questions, or even to take up a definite political and economic position, than it is to create a new style of life (*Presence of the Kingdom*, p. 145).

Christian proclamation must become incarnational in the practical, daily realities of the believer's life in the world. Ellul goes on to say that there is no longer any Christian style of life in the world. The problem is not that Christians have no style of life, but that there is no longer any distinctively Christian style of life. Instead, the style of life most prevalent in our congregations is one which has been accepted and adopted from the dominant values of society and culture.

. . . they have many individual virtues, but they have no style of life, or rather, they have exactly that which has been imposed upon them by their sociological conditions; that is to say, by their class, their nation, their environment, and so on. It is not their *spiritual* condition which affects their style of life; it is their political or economic condition . . . (*Presence of the Kingdom*, p. 146).

So, the environmental facts of our lives have become more determinative of our style of life than our identity as Christians. This problem is most crucial, for, in a situation of widespread social conformity, the life-style of those in the churches becomes evidence for the view, held by many, that the gospel does not transform people's lives but is a mere appendage which provides religious sanction and justification to lives really lived on other grounds.

Christian life-style begins with a break with the world situation and its givens. It is a choice of a path which leads the Christian out of conformity to the world. Therefore, it is the choice of a path moving in a different direction from those who persist in conformity and uniformity with the patterns and structures of the world system. The path of obedience to Christ brings a break in the human situation made possible by the intrusion of the gospel as the new factor which breaks the dominance of the old factors of the world. The gospel signals the end of the uncontested dominion of the principalities and powers of the world over people's lives. All this has been brought about by the inbreaking of the kingdom. Only our daily decisions and choices can show the reality of our relationship to Jesus Christ. Those around us will only be convinced that the gospel is indeed a radical alternative to the values and structures of the world when that claim is confirmed by our personal and corporate obedience.

The call to discipleship always involves a break with established norms and values, with the prevailing assumptions and idolatries of the present order. Various authorities, institutions, political and economic powers, historical forces, ideological necessities, and social facts become idolatrous by demanding an absolute kind of allegiance and value and by coming between God and his people and by coming between people. If we believe Christ has freed us from the rule of these idols and powers of the world, we are enabled, indeed, are commanded to demonstrate our freedom from them. The demonstration of freedom in the world, by his disciples, is nothing less than the declaration of the victory of Christ in history. The many who still suffer under the rule of the powers and idols must be able to see that their absolute dominion and control have been broken. Karl Barth in *Church Dogmatics* speaks of "The Call of Discipleship."

The break made by God in Jesus must become history. This is why Jesus calls His disciples. And it is for this reason that His disciples cannot be content with a mere theory about the relativisation of those false absolutes; a mere attitude of mind in which these gods no longer exist for them; an inward freedom in relation to them. It is for this reason that in different ways they are called out in practice from these attachments, and it is a denial of the call to discipleship if they evade the achievement of acts and attitudes in which externally and visibly they break free from these attachments (vol. 4, part 2, pp. 543–53).

Because the victory of Christ must be visibly and concretely demonstrated in history, a mere profession of inward or "spiritual" freedom in relation to the dominant powers and idols of the world is inadequate and useless as a witness to the kingdom of God. It is essential that those in the world see some signs and manifestations of what has occurred in the life of the believer. The disciple of Christ is a sign in history of what God has accomplished in Jesus Christ. That is the nature of our calling. The call is to come out from our former allegiance and servitude to those things which have been defeated by Christ's victory. While it is true that this demonstration of freedom will take different forms in different times and circumstances, it is certain that it must always take concrete forms which make the victory of Christ visible and meaningful. Our obedience must necessarily consist in public and visible nonconformity which embraces specific attitudes and acts, demonstrating opposition to these powers and idols and thereby witnessing to Christ's victory over them. The follower of Christ will always seek to translate his or her conversion into actual forms of living.

Barth cautions against easing the requirements of Christian lifestyle:

We will always know that it is His voice which calls us from the fact that in what is demanded of us we shall always have to do with the great self-evident factors of our environments, and therefore of the world as a whole, which will have to be made in fact, both outwardly and inwardly, along the lines indicated in the New Testament [He lists the breaks with the attachment to money and possessions, with violence and power, with fame, with family, and with religion], corresponding to, and attesting, the eruption of the kingdom of God. . . . There can certainly be no question of a deviation from these main lines. . . . And there will always be reason for distrust against ourselves if we think that what may be required of us along these lines will be easier, or more comfortable than what was required of them. Grace . . . cannot have become more cheap today; it may well have become more costly (vol. 4, part 2, pp. 543–53).

All this means that everything about our lives must be placed in the light of our faith in Christ and the efficacy of the kingdom of God. The gospel gives us different priorities from those of the popular culture and offers us a different agenda from that of the political economy. It effects a reversal of accepted definitions and initiates the process of redirection. It makes possible a fundamental break with the prevailing idolatries and establishes an alternative mode of power in the world.

Christian radicalism means to be rooted in Christ and to judge one's life and social environment in light of the reality of the kingdom of God. It is to continually scrutinize all social and political "givens" and to challenge all that conflicts with obedience to Christ. Christian radicalism is not a strategy but the result of transformation. A Christian is more than someone who wants to change things; a Christian is someone who is being changed. The process of change begins as we give ourselves over to Christ. It involves giving up our right to ourselves and depending upon God. The key to the kingdom is faithfulness in following Christ daily. Therefore, the Christian style of life is not an objective but a consequence of obedience and witness. The Christian life-style is a life of testimony.

You are the salt to the world. And if salt becomes tasteless, how is its saltness to be restored? It is now good for nothing but to be thrown away and trodden underfoot.

You are light for all the world. A town that stands on a hill cannot be hidden. When a lamp is lit, it is not put under the mealtub, but on the lamp-stand, where it gives light to everyone in the house. And you, like the lamp, must shed light among your fellows, so that, when they see the good you do, they may give praise to your Father in heaven (Matt. 5:13–16, NEB).

There is something potentially explosive about a serious commitment to the gospel of Jesus Christ. Every evangelist runs the risk that the seed of the gospel, once planted in the life of a new believer, may grow into a dynamic force which threatens to overturn the very status quo in which the evangelist finds comfort and rest. That is to say, the gospel cannot be forever controlled nor suppressed and rendered harmless by the rich and powerful. The biblical promise is that the message of Christ will continue to penetrate and ultimately transform the human condition.

The transforming dynamic of the gospel can seem very obscured and almost obliterated when the church eases the tension between the claims of Christ and the claims of the world and seeks to put the gospel into more manageable molds and categories. Conformity can go on for generations at a time, but, as the history of the church testifies, the explosive power of the gospel will always be recovered and felt again when men and women have their eyes and lives opened to the living Christ and proclaim with Peter, "We shall obey God rather than men."

2. Returning to Our Roots

Conformity—the Enemy

> ... present your bodies as a living sacrifice, holy and acceptable to God, which is your spiritual worship. Do not be conformed to this world but be transformed by the renewal of your mind, that you may prove what is the will of God, what is good and acceptable and perfect (Rom. 12:1, 2, RSV).

Or, to offer a free paraphrase:

> Put your bodies where your doctrines are, by the consistent worship that demands your very self as a living sacrifice, and stop allowing yourselves to be conformed and schematized by the world-system. Instead of being squeezed into its mold, have your minds transformed and keep letting yourselves be metamorphosized by the renewal of your world-view and your moral disposition, so that you may be able to discern, recognize, approve, and enjoy the will of God.

Conformity to the world's patterns and mindset is the deadly enemy of the church. Pressure to accept the values, assumptions, loyalties, myths, goals, necessities, and givens of the world's cultural and ideological systems continually threatens the witness and mission of the church. Submitting to that pressure inevitably results in the compromise and conformity that fashions the church after the spirit of the age rather than after the Spirit of Christ. The teaching of this passage is that we are *already* conformed to the world. The values of the surrounding environment have become our own. The question, then, is not how we can keep from becoming conformed. The real question is how we can be *transformed*. The unexamined conformity which comes to infect the church is here being challenged by the apostle.

In this instruction to the Roman Christians, the tense of the verbs used suggests that the task of nonconformity is continual, never consummated, never attained. As the efforts of the world to squeeze the church into its mold are unceasing, so the commitment of the Christian community to nonconformity with present patterns of the world system must be perpetual.

Also clear in the biblical passage is that conformity and nonconformity are related to moral discernment and ethical sensitivity. Here Paul teaches that our willingness to break from the patterns of the world, by allowing our minds and very natures to be transformed, is essential to the ability to properly discern the will of God. Thus, the church's nonconformity to the world is crucial to its self-understanding and faithfulness to its mission in the world, "to know what is good, acceptable, and perfect." Conversely, a church whose life is characterized by mindless conformity cannot understand God's will and becomes ethically blinded by its misplaced and false identification with the world. This is the situation in which the church finds itself today.

According to the apostle, transformation occurs as we offer our very selves as a "living sacrifice" which is a requirement of acceptable worship to God. Proper worship in this context has clear ethical implications and can never be separated from the obedient life of the church. Thus, the Christian community must always examine how the world would enslave it to conformity and command obedience from it by stamping the body of Christ with the image of the world.

A principal and widespread cause of unbelief in our generation is the cultural conformity of the church with its consequent ethical hypocrisy and paralysis. For many, it is not the gospel that is incredible but the church that is. Failure to show forth the reality of salvation and transformation results in a meaningless proclamation on the part of the church. Most outside the church have heard the words, "Jesus saves" or "Jesus is Lord," but few have any notion of what the words mean or what they might have to do with the practical affairs of human life and society. In failing to demonstrate the reality of its proclamation with the credibility of its own life, the church's words strike many as confusing and without authority. A church that is captive to its culture and merely echoes the values of the larger society cannot be prophetic or truly evangelistic.

When being a Christian becomes an easy and comfortable affair, there develops a rather broad credibility gap between the doctrinal profession of the church and its ethical practice. Salvation and church membership are offered as rather cost-free items marketed to people unwilling to have their lives radically changed. Criticism directed against the practice of the Christian community is more difficult to counter than an assault on the theology and belief of the church. For often it is not an intellectual assault that can be answered by the church's systems of apologetic defenses. The greatest need in such a situation is for an *ethical apologetic*, a practiced demonstration of the meaning and power of the church's biblical theology. In the Romans passage, Paul teaches that the only acceptable response in a situation of conformity is a recovery of the requirements of true and spiritual worship. The connections between worship and ethics, between worship and politics, will be taken up later. First, however, we must examine some contemporary types of conformity which have infected the church and compromised a biblical witness.

Civil Religion

It has become common practice for Christians to identify closely with the cultural and sociopolitical systems which surround them. This practice often degenerates into what many have called a civil religion which blesses the established status quo instead of calling it into question. In affluent societies, many

Christian groups and churches have particularly identified with wealth and power. The rich and powerful of both church and state have actively fostered this special relationship and have benefited from it. Our churches have been guilty of misplaced allegiance and often outright idolatry to the extent that they have failed to distinguish between the gods of civil religion and the God who reveals himself in Scripture and supremely in Jesus Christ. Civil religion, in contrast to biblical faith, is devoid of moral content and carries with it little capacity to bring a word of judgment or correction to a social order. On the contrary, its function is to provide religious justification for the social order, to serve as the ideological glue which holds the society together in consensus and conformity.

Thus, civil religion is easily manipulated to serve the needs of power. It is most often used by power to give a religious dimension and credibility to policy decisions reached on other grounds. This civil religion often results in the disastrous equation of the Christian way of life with the way of life promoted by nations, economic systems, or ideological doctrines. The idolatrous equation of Christian faith with the national consensus or with political systems and movements is a theological error that occurs along the entire political spectrum and is limited neither to the right nor to the left. Civil religion and the confusing of it with Christian faith is both useful to those in power and heretical from a biblical standpoint because it elevates cultural norms, political ideology, and the state in particular to the level of ultimate concern, which is idolatry. Biblical faith brings a word of judgment and correction to any culture or political system and suggests that the state is never to be made an object of religious loyalty.

Civil religion has a catalytic relationship to nationalism and is most pronounced when nationalism has assumed aggressive, expansionist, and missionary proportions. Nationalism as an ideology is in conflict with biblical norms in its assigning more worth and importance to one people and nation over others. As such, it is an affront to the work of Christ which shatters the barriers and divisions imposed by a fallen humanity to separate from each other, to scorn and oppress each other, to fight and kill each other, all to maintain and pursue the national identity and purpose. Often, civil religion has provided the religious cover for the most destructive impulses of a nation that comes to regard itself as having a special place or preferred status in the divine plan for the world.

Civil religion promotes an uncritical stance in regard to the state and to political ideology generally. It falsely eases the proper tension between the demands of biblical faith and the values and assumptions of any social order or political system. The church must always maintain this tension in relation to those values and assumptions if it is to retain its prophetic integrity and capacity. The mistake in dropping a critical stance, in easing this necessary tension, occurs across the political spectrum and is more a theological error than merely a political mistake. Governments and movements of both right and left seek to bring the church into the political struggle to support their interests and to provide a theological rationale and religious motivation for their partisan causes. Much theological distortion occurs in this process, and the critical and corrective values of true biblical faith are sacrificed on the altar of ideological necessity. Christians tend easily to forget that Jesus Christ is a stranger to any culture, an unwanted disrupter of any ideological system. The civil religion of the established order is always resisted by those groups in opposition until their own regime and ideological preferences gain power and their own forms of civil religion become established.

Civil religion encourages people, even the people of God, to look to the state, the nation, the ideology, or political messiahs for their social salvation. Though God works through nations and movements, usually in spite of themselves, the primary instrument of God's purposes in history is meant to be the faithfulness of a called forth and gathered people as they obediently respond to God's will. The state and the political process are not the bearers of ultimate value and meaning in the biblical scheme of things.

Civil religion is inherently a false religion because it is the religious expression and incarnation of the dominant values and assumptions of the present order that is passing away—values and assumptions that live in sharp contrast to the priorities of the kingdom of God. When conformity to such false religion infects the churches, the very meaning of the gospel may be lost or blurred as those in the congregations become unable to make a choice or even perceive the need to make a choice between God and Caesar. The transforming dynamic of the gospel and the prophetic cutting edge of biblical faith is exchanged for a nationalistic and ideological faith that enjoys the fruits of success and power. Thus crippled with prophetic impotence, the church begins to render unto Caesar all that Caesar asks rather than only what is due him. The church makes an uneasy bargain to "stick to spiritual matters" and to the preaching of a "pure" gospel stripped of its power to make converts into active disciples, stripped of its danger to the status quo.

In recent times, we have seen the eagerness of powerful and repressive governments to cooperate with such a church. The state becomes anxious to invite church leaders to mingle in the circles of power, anxious to support its evangelism which has been rendered harmless and congenial to the governing authorities. If the church will incorporate the values of "good citizenship" and "obedience to authority" into its evangelistic proclamation, the state may even become an active promoter of the church's evangelism while giving to its leaders the preferred status of spiritual advisor to power. The leaders of church and state may then join together in ceremony and celebration which give honor to the state and provide a religious sense and meaning to its history, experience, and national purpose.

In such a situation, the church loses touch with its very identity. Genuine Christian commitment comes to mean less and less as a motivating power in people's lives and as a source of prophetic judgment and social liberation. The proclamation of the church degenerates into a caricature of Christianity—enculturated, domesticated, lifeless. It is not merely the rich and powerful or the ideological partisans who have fostered this false religion. The system is indeed guilty, but we all are implicated to the extent that the system's values have become our own.

• The church does not exist to sanctify and provide the base of support for any social order. Rather, the Christian community must be that body of people that continually scrutinizes the political consensus and the cultural and ideological norms upon which the social order is founded. Prevailing attitudes and social values must be evaluated in contrast to the kingdom of God and a biblical word of judgment and correction brought to bear on the situation. The church, when most obedient to its calling, is a stranger, an exile, an alien, seeking to sing the Lord's song in a strange land. The obedient church is necessarily a minority phenomenon because it is composed of people with a view of life that makes them poor, exposed, full of risk—a threat to any cultural or political status quo. The bible shows God moving in history, continually calling his people away from the idolatries they have erected for themselves to avoid dependence on their Lord, away from the false gods around them that they have come to worship. The New Testament confronts us with Christ, the Word made flesh, the one who is free from the power of idolatries and free even from the power of death itself. That one who is free offers freedom to his followers who would seek first his kingdom and its righteousness. Freedom comes in and through Christ as our lives are changed from service to the idolatries that surround us to obedience to his lordship. The Christian community is a people freed to reject the patterns of the present world system and the idolatrous values and assumptions upon which it is based, freed to bear witness by their life together to the new possibilities of the kingdom of God which is nothing less than the inbreaking of a new order to replace the old.

Because the early Christians would not worship the imperial cult of the Roman empire, they were often accused of atheism. In other words, the early church was atheistic in regard to the gods of the empire. The question must be asked, Is the church today atheistic in regard to the gods of the American system, or does it offer the homage and worship that those false gods demand? To be a Christian is to be an atheist to all the gods of this world and to their manifestations in every historical system and ideological consensus. To be an atheist to the gods of the American system, to give ourselves over to those whom that system treats as enemies and outsiders, will bring persecution and the danger of death itself.

It should come as no surprise that major religious movements also become conformed and coopted by the prevailing cultural and political winds. In our own times, movements of both conservative and liberal religion have been much too eager to meet the world on its own terms. Despite their theological polarities and expressed hostilities toward each other, they have both tended to define the meaning of Christian faith according to the world views and life-styles each has adopted from the secular culture. In each case, the *whole* deposit of revelation is neglected or selectively appropriated, and conformity is the inevitable result.

Conservative Religion

Conservative religion has often produced a cultural theology that fosters an acceptance or at least an aquiescence to the cultural and political status quo. Jesus is proclaimed as savior, but the implications of his lordship over all of life are not often drawn out or are spiritualized into irrelevance. The influence of individualism and the ethic of success in evangelism has resulted in a depreciation of Jesus' call for public discipleship. The heresy of grace without discipleship has come to characterize the evangelistic proclamations of conservative religion.

As we have previously noted, an individualistic world view, adopted from secular culture, has fostered a misunderstanding of both sin and the gospel which are seen in Scripture as having individual and corporate dimensions. When this occurs, evil is viewed for the most part in personal terms and is not connected to the infliction of evil by social systems and institutional arrangements. Salvation, too, is wrongly viewed as an exclusively private and personal affair and thus separated from its social and political meaning. There has been a marked tendency in conservative religious circles to put religion and politics into dichotomy, which invariably results in conformity with the status quo either by intent or default.

In contrast to biblical thought, personal realities are divorced from institutional and social realities, and the vital connections between them are not made. Such practice narrows the scope and meaning of the gospel and causes ethical blindness and insensitivity. Our lives are lived either in support of present social and political realities or in opposition to them, but never in neutrality.

Combined with these theological errors, conservative religion has increased its conformity by joining with liberal religion in identification with the values and life-style of the affluent middle and upper classes of technocratic social orders. It is discernible from Scripture and history that the early church had a very different class make-up than do the congregations of our churches today. A narrow and distorted view of the world is inevitable in a church that has become so tied to the world view of the affluent classes and segments of the social order. Since most of the world is poor and wretched, a church that is comfortable and affluent and is tied to the wealthy classes cannot hope to understand the world in which it is called to minister. Poor theological judgment and biblical interpretation can easily degenerate into idolatrous relationships with political and economic power. Jacques Ellul comments on the biblical priority:

The place of the Nazarene's followers is not with the oppressor but with the oppressed, not with the mighty but the weak, not with the overfed but with the hungry, not with the free but the enslaved, not with the opulent but the poverty stricken, not with the well but with the sick, not with the successful but the defeated, not with the comfortable majority but with the miserable minorities, not with the bourgeois but with the proletariat (quoted in Vernon Grounds, *Revolution and the Christian Faith*, p. 216).

The concern for sound doctrine among religious conservatives can become dead orthodoxy when not related to a style of life and action consistent with what is believed. Many who would accept the authority of the Bible doctrinally, balk at the more exacting demands of Scripture for social justice and for an incarnational life-style, a way of practical living that gives reality to the power of biblical theology. It is clear that true faith and spirituality transform the conditions of life into which the message of the Scripture comes. The life of one touched by the gospel must reflect the concern of God for justice, healing, and peace in a broken world.

The Bible teaches that personal faith divorced from an active commitment to social justice is a mockery of the gospel. The Law of Moses contained special provisions for redistributing wealth and providing for the poor. Amos, Isaiah, Jeremiah, Hosea, and Micah rebuked oppressive affluence and exploitive power and demanded social justice and righteousness that brought judgment to the social order. The psalmist saw God vindicating the cause of the poor and triumphing over the rich and powerful.

John the Baptist's call for repentance involved divesting personal wealth and sharing with the poor. The promise of the gospel to Mary announces personal and social revolution in its heralding of a whole new order in human affairs. Jesus begins his ministry anointed by the Spirit "to preach good news to the poor ... to proclaim release to the captives and recovering of sight to the blind, to set at liberty those who are oppressed, to proclaim the acceptable year of the Lord." He later tells us that our profession of love for God will be concretely tested by our actions in feeding the hungry, clothing the naked, caring for the homeless, and ministering to the practical needs of the afflicted. "As you have done to the least of these, you have done to me." John says that if we say we love God and fail to demonstrate that love by closing our lives to those in need, we are liars. James proclaims that faith without works is dead and warns the rich of the judgment that is coming upon them. Paul describes the cosmic and political implications of a resurrected Lord who has won the victory over the fallen powers and principalities of the world systems that hold people captive, thus breaking their absolute dominion and assuring their final defeat.

Liberal Religion

Liberal religion has often produced a secular theology which also has become a conformist religion. The lack of biblical foundations, the eroding of transcendence in theology, the depreciation of personal conversion and commitment, and the uncritical conformity to contemporary social and political options and trends have led to a secularization in liberal religion and a conformity as real as that of the cultural theology of conservative religion.

The cost of moving away from solid biblical rootage has been paid in the loss of clear Christian initiative and distinctiveness. Without a firm basis in revelation, the theological agenda can only be derived from the changing assumptions, thought forms, and social movements of secular culture. In such a situation, theology comes, for the most part, to mirror the secular mindset or perhaps to provide an unconvincing religious dimension and interpretation to it. Critical theological reflection and insight is sacrificed when we limit ourselves to the options posed by various ideological contestants in the secular marketplace. When biblical theology is neglected, when the meaning and importance of revelation becomes blurred, the church becomes completely dependent on the world to define the nature of its mission. The inevitable consequence is conformity and compromise with the patterns of the present world in their various cultural and political expressions. The particular insight that the Word of God can bring to the social situation is missed when the church rushes to take sides in struggles where the battle lines have already been drawn by others.

Liberal religion has been too easily intimidated by secular and naturalistic assumptions. In the effort to become acceptable and meaningful to the modern mind, we run the danger of forfeiting the very word that the modern mind needs most to hear. Christian faith undergoes reductions through a filtering process that sifts the gospel through the grid of secular systems or world views. The process of "demythologizing" the content of the gospel has often served to deny its reality and power. The consequences of such demythologizing have often been a degeneration to a rootless religion without the ability to offer spiritual life and resources in the resolutions of human problems.

Liberal religion has too often depreciated the meaning of conversion and the necessity of evangelism, thus losing the dynamic of personal commitment in relation to Christ which is foundational to Christian witness and action in the world. Without a clear understanding of the meaning of personal encounter with Jesus Christ, the theological task becomes absurd and merely academic. Many seminarians can describe the language and history of every verse of the Sermon on the Mount or the third chapter of John but have no understanding of the meaning of the passages for their lives. When people are searching for something that will change their lives, all that may be offered to them is commitment to the institutions of the church itself rather than the gospel.

When important decisions are actually made, both conservative and liberal religion have capitulated to culture through outright political conformity or by the endless pursuing of changing fads and styles with no discernible roots in the gospel. Our churches need to be deoriented from the doctrines of conservative, liberal, and civil religion by being transformed biblically.

Revelation and Resistance

What the world happens to consider meaningful must never define the content of God's revelation to us. The world has not the right to assign Christ his place in it. We must recognize that a true word from God will always be offensive and disrupting to those who have defined their lives autonomously. God's revelation will never seem congenial to the presuppositions of secular society and culture. The last thing that the competing religious and political factions of Israel wanted to accept was Jesus of Nazareth and his gospel of the kingdom. He was an offense to both the religious and the political establishment and to its Zealot opposition, an unwelcomed addition to the range of opinion and options that had been constructed. A faithful proclamation and demonstration of the Word of God will always have this offensive and disruptive quality and must not be distorted and redefined to make it more acceptable to the reigning cultural, intellectual, or political consensus.

The power of an affluent technological society to co-opt movements, including its opposition, is not to be underestimated. Movements spawned by the injustice and alienation of the present order may serve for a time as the conscience of a nation and the focal point of resistance to the cultural and political consensus. But most end up exhausting themselves, crumbling without adequate foundations, and being ground down by the counterforce of a social order with the long-range power to bring most things into conformity, including its opposition. The price of obedience and conformity is a loss of conscience; the rewards of compliance are success, security, and a numbing affluence.

Most would-be alternatives fail to take seriously the need for fundamental redirection and radical change. Belief in the marginal reform, social readjustment and engineering, and evolutionary progress has shown itself to be inadequate and counterproductive. Most ideological competitors accept the basic values and patterns of the system and have their securities there. The system easily absorbs new movements, styles, and initiatives that do not threaten its core assumptions or undermine its existence. A genuine alternative must not take the normal patterns of the present world system as its starting point but should be rooted outside that system if it is to be able to meaningfully challenge the assumptions and values of the present order. That is precisely the hope that comes from a recovery of biblical faith in theology, the rediscovery of revelation in the historic Christian sense.

If theology is to be revolutionary in its impact, it must be revelational in its basis. Theology becomes confused and distorted when it loses its starting point in revelation. Many years ago, Dietrich Bonhoeffer described the theological task with clarity: "From God to reality, not from reality to God, goes the path of theology." In other words, the Christian message does not originate in human life and society but must come to them. The struggle of the church will always be to receive and witness to the revelation of God in its own period of history. The church must preserve the wholeness and integrity of revelation against any attempt to reduce its meaning or redefine it by suppressing those parts of it which conflict with the contemporary world view. Most Christians today suffer from a constricting conformity to one ideological option or another rather than employing discernment in how the Word of God can be brought to bear in a given situation. Through the changes of history and culture, the revelation of God as declared in Scripture continues to bring an authentic message which penetrates the human situation and overturns human speculation and ideas about what is true, meaningful, and credible. The fundamental question now, as always, is whether the Word of God has been received and obeyed.

The hope of meaningful countercultural resistance to any social or political consensus is not to be found in depreciating transcendence and moving in secular directions. That practice has, in fact, become a formula for conformity. On the contrary, the church's proper role as an alternative corporate reality and prophetic presence in any social order will be recovered only as the people of God return to their biblical roots and stand firmly on the ground of revelation.

Biblical faith is subversive. The church can only provide a radical opposition when it defines itself outside of the system by being firmly rooted in the revelation of God's Word. Being so rooted, its life need no longer be defined entirely by the present. The church begins to find its identity in the kingdom of God and to resist being co-opted by the artificial values of the present system. The Christian claim is that the transcendent has become flesh in Jesus Christ who lived and taught the will of God on earth. The proclamation of judgment on the present world system and the offer of salvation in Christ have never been popular messages. When the people of God are the most obedient to God's revelation and the most faithful to their biblical basis, they are the most scandalous and the most threatening to the established order. Christian resistance is based in the revelation of God in Scripture and in the incarnation of Jesus Christ. It is empowered in the present by the presence of the Holy Spirit as promised by Christ and is motivated by confident hope in the coming kingdom.

Close attention to the nature, structure, and operational characteristics of cultural and social systems must be linked to a serious study of the Bible, a life of prayer, and a deep experience of worship. As Karl Barth once suggested, we need to practice theology with our Bibles in one hand and our newspapers in the other. Often in the past and present, when political power has reached totalitarian proportions, Bible study, prayer, and worship have become focal points of resistance to the established order.

Our churches need to be deoriented from the patterns of the present order and transformed biblically. The church must again become pilgrim and prophet—a community in the process of continual disentanglement from the values that dominate the age. It must be sensitive to the blind spots that mold its thinking and shape its actions when it is peacefully co-existing with the standard that is passing away. It must proclaim the great refusal to be squeezed into the world's pattern and must pledge allegiance to the coming reign of God.

With the willingness to hear and the courage to obey the witness of Scripture, the church can recapture its identity and mission in the world, which is to be a sign of Christ's presence. This makes the Christian community a countersign to the status quo, a scandal to the established order. By recovering the biblical tension between its own life and the life of the world, the church can again become a source of judgment and correction to the prevailing patterns of its age.

In doing so, we may be able to transcend the polarities between conservative and liberal religion and forge a biblically based faith which can speak with clarity and authority to the issues of life as we confront them in our own times. In the face of a society whose affluence keeps others in hunger and misery, the church must become poor. In the face of a world system embroiled in a violent striving for power, the church must become a suffering servant. In the face of a society of mass alienation and fragmenting isolation, the church must be a healing community of reconciliation. In the face of a social order dependent upon docility and conformity, the church must become an agent of resistance and change.

3. Idols, Powers, and Worship

Idolatry

When I was involved in radical student movements, I believed, along with most other young activists, that our problems were due to malice on the part of the national leadership and ignorance on the part of the public. We felt that the evils we opposed resided with the policymakers, and that "the people" would make basic changes if they could be informed about what was really going on. I no longer believe that. Rather, the issues that confront us, the human atrocities that plead for change, are due to more than lack of information, education, and technology. The injustice, the violence, the inhumanity, the painful afflictions of human life and society have to do with moral and spiritual questions on which choices are made each day by both national leaders and populations.

These choices have a great deal to do with what the Bible refers to as idolatry. The worship of idols is one of the most consistent themes throughout all of Scripture. While the word *idolatry* conjures up all sorts of images of ancient pagan rituals and cults, the Bible sees idolatry as present and pervasive in every culture, nation, and period of history.

The worship of idols takes many forms, some direct and unmistakable, some far more deceptive and subtle. In our own times, we witness persons, relationships, institutions, ideologies, movements, and nations caught in the grip of contemporary idolatries. The contemporary idolatries that have captured our worship and servitude are familiar realities; money, possessions, power, race, class, sex, nation, status, success, work, violence, religion, ideology, causes, and so on. The militant power of the contemporary idolatries has captured the corporations and institutions of commerce, the state and the branches of government, the private and public bureaucracies, the various professions, the schools and universities, media and entertainment, and the churches. The presence of these idols or gods is deeply felt in our economic and political systems, our social and cultural patterns, crucially affecting the way we relate to one another. Idols perpetuate themselves by erecting self-justifying ideologies and informational systems with the seeming ability to turn falsehood into truth by the distortion of language itself.

Biblically understood, idolatry originates in the human decision to seek life and salvation apart from the source of life in God. In fact, idols are "imposters of God," as William Stringfellow has described them. They may be things, ideas, persons or institutions exalted and worshiped as gods. Idolatry makes men and women subservient and submissive to things; this dehumanizes human life. Rather than these finite realities serving people, people come to serve and worship them as gods, which is idolatry. They come to command worship as objects of ultimate concern. Things, institutions, ideas, concepts, or persons are allowed to substitute for God. Idolatry denies the place of God as the giver of life and the author of salvation, dehumanizes people by making them pay homage to objects not deserving of worship, and denigrates the proper vocation of things meant to be servants of human life, not masters over it.

Idolatry is a decision to seek life and salvation by the worship and trust of something other than God. It is to identify with some part of one's environment, a part of reality that is within reach and seems to have the power to bring the satisfaction and fulfillment that is missing in one's life. Having given up the possibilities of trusting God, trust is placed in something that can, it is believed, be manipulated and possessed. The mode of salvation thus becomes self-appropriation and consumption and depends upon a personal identification with something that can be manipulated—

an idol. This style of life is what the Bible calls living in darkness and sin and is ultimately centered around the consumptive possibilities for oneself and the illusion of being able to manipulate and control one's idols rather than being manipulated and controlled by them.

One may choose material security and comfort, power and domination over others, human recognition, gratification of the senses, particular kinds of experiences, and so on. But whatever the choice, there is never enough to satisfy, to fill the void, to bring fullness and fulfillment. One always needs more because more of the self always needs to be filled up. Because most others have also adopted the life-style of salvation by self-appropriation, consumption, and manipulation, they are viewed as competitors, as people who have the capacity of depriving one of one's salvation and fulfillment. The objects sought in this process take on personal and ultimate value while the persons involved become mere objects in the struggle. Seeking salvation apart from the source of life, failing in the attempt to save oneself by consumption and manipulation, and accepting the necessity of viewing others as competitors, results in alienation—alienation from God, from others, from oneself.

Idolatry, and its consequent alienation, is ultimately the worship of death itself. William Stringfellow comments:

The term "death" is being used here in the manifold connotations of its uses in the Bible; not only physical death but all forms of diminution of human life and development and dignity, and all forms of alienation of men from themselves and from one another and from God. Since idolatry of any kind demeans man, prevents him from being fully human, death is that which, under many disguises, idolaters really worship. On the other hand, justification by faith means that the integrity of human life as a gift is radically affirmed. Man is set free from enslavement to the work of his hands or his mind to pursue his human vocation, to live and live more fully in relationship to himself and other men and to the whole of creation (*Imposters of God*, p. 29).

The cycle and its destructive consequences are no less true for institutions than for individuals. Institutions, rather than developing as corporate bodies in service of human life and well-being, become distorted by the purposes of appropriation and manipulation. Distorted institutions project responsibility for their failures onto others, and any who won't accept the plan of salvation offered by the institution or who stand in the way of it are designated as "enemy." Identification with an institution comes when its purposes are seen to be continuous or contributive to one's own. Identification is made, not only with a particular institution, but with the political, economic, and sociocultural system on which the institution is dependent and forms a part. The fulfillment of oneself is seen to be dependent upon the maintenance and perpetuation of those institutions. This, of course, is idolatry. Breaking the cycle of idolatry requires salvation through relationship with the source of life itself, which can bring freedom from the identification with idols and from viewing others as competitors and threats to one's own salvation. When the source of one's salvation is beyond oneself, one is free to serve rather than to appropriate. The life and death of Christ demonstrate that salvation and reconciliation come through conquering alienation by love and a cross. Through self-giving servanthood, the Christian community demonstrates the victory of Christ over human alienation and begins to break the hold of the prevailing idolatries over people's lives.

The Fall

America is a fallen nation. In fact, the fall is the principal political and spiritual fact of America and other nation-states. That is what the Bible teaches and what the churches refuse to believe. If we had believed the Bible at this point, we would not be so inclined to ignore the violence and oppression inflicted upon the poor, upon racial minorities, and upon those whom the nation designates as enemies. We would not have chosen to resist the facts of atrocities like Vietnam. We would certainly not have been surprised by the cancer of political corruption and the totalitarian spirit revealed in the Watergate conspiracies and in the repressive behavior of government security organizations. The moral insanity, the falsehood, the injustice, the violence, the chaos, and the brutality that has come to characterize the United States and other powerful nation-states can be more adequately explained by the biblical teaching of the fall than by mere ideological analyses and explanations. The Bible teaches that the whole of creation has become alienated from God and, thereby, from itself. The biblical description of the fall and its consequence in alienation is pervasive, affecting not only persons and their relationships but also institutions, nations, governments, corporations, ideologies, systems, bureaucracies, movements, idols—all those structural realities that are biblically referred to as *principalities and powers*. On the other hand, the church's understanding of the fall is naïve, narrow, misinformed, and biblically spurious. Indeed, the preaching and the practice of most of our churches serve to deny the reality of the fall or, perhaps, to claim a special exemption from the fall for their nation, preferred institutions, or favorite idols.

Many Americans are uncomfortable with the suggestion that their own nation bears major responsibility for the sufferings of people. They recoil when their country is accused of economic and cultural imperialism, military aggression, or the exercise of mass violence and genocide for selfish interests. They are angered by the charge that their social order is founded upon a self-righteous sense of national destiny, upon white supremacy, upon a preference for property values over human values. They are defensive of their society's dominant economic and political institutions when such institutions are exposed for maintaining and perpetuating injustice. They reject the notion that their nation utilizes propaganda to justify itself or resorts to various forms of control, repression, coercion, naked force, and, ultimately, death when necessary to advance its purposes or to protect and extend its authority and power.

Many would rather retreat to the more comfortable belief that their nation, their system, their "side," acts out of righteous or, at worse, mistaken motivations; that its basic values, purposes, institutions, and intentions are honorable and noble (for example, that our nation acts only to protect freedom and self-determination, that what is best for business or for the party is best for all, that our military might is only to protect the peace, that here the people decide, that anyone can succeed with hard work, and so on). These and other social mythologies have characterized many nation-states and have been most pronounced in those which have been most violent and destructive.

The basic flaw in such thinking is not primarily political. In other words, the question is deeper and more profound than "correct" political analysis. The primary problem is biblical and comes from a misreading of Scripture. It derives from the theological naïveté of failing to take the fall seriously. Such faulty insight results from the secularization of a church that has forgotten its biblical roots and fallen into idolatry.

A recognition of the fall and its pervasive consequences for human life and society is a prerequisite for comprehending biblical politics. No longer can we avoid a more profound understanding of the operational facts of our nation-states and social institutions. We have seen enough of the exercise of abusive power to make future atrocities allowed by our ignorance inexcusable. The course of recent events serves to document that those who make policy at the highest levels of power are deliberate about and conscious of their calculations and decisions. A careful reading of the New Testament suggests that the spiritual forces that come to dominate institutions of power eventually dominate those who seek to rule and "lord it over" the people. Naïveté, mistaken idealism, public concern, and sentimentality can no longer be said to be the underlying and determining characteristics of power. Painful confrontation with the nature and reality of the powers of the world system must begin to change the relationship of the church to those powers. We must begin to counter conscious deception and official falsehood. Language itself has become distorted by the needs of power and loses its relationship to reality ("peace with honor," "protective reaction," "national security," "free enterprise," "peoples' republic," "pacification," "law and order," "freedom of religion," and so on).

The American public has developed an amazing capacity for tolerating contradiction; perhaps that is part of the price of empire. The ironies of it would be almost humorous were it not for the victims—those who suffer the consequences of American contradictions. The public grants extraordinary authority and power to the economic and political managers and gets, in exchange, unprecedented affluence and a protected sense of national pride and destiny. The nation is thus able to stay on top of the world heap and still hear its leaders continue to talk of our commitments to self-determination and freedom. The government is able to kill a million Indochinese and justify it with "saving them from communism," or "containing the Chinese threat," or "protecting American lives," or "destroying a village to save it," or "not backing out of our commitments," or "bringing our prisoners home with their heads high," depending on the year of the war and the official administration line. The nation's leaders are exposed lying, cheating, and stealing while still keeping down the poor and repressing dissent to "preserve law and order." The United States is able to subsidize dozens of dictatorships and still be the leader of the Free World. The American people are able to gobble up half the world's consumable resources and still "praise God from whom all blessings flow." In such a situation, the prophetic function of "truth-telling" is a central part of responsible biblical faith.

New understanding and awareness of the nature of power and the structure of our societies is necessary to know how and where to oppose the infliction of institutional evil and suffering at home and abroad. Such understanding will come through a study of the Bible and of political and social conditions and events. The attainment of such insight after the appalling ignorance and apathy of the postwar period is essential in making social change and in restoring a sense of Christian integrity. It seems increasingly clear that the brutalizing and destructive consequences of the forceful exercise of power will not be accepted either by the victims, or by the absolute demands and judgments of a moral God.

The Powers

The destructive meaning of idolatry and the fall is very relevant to institutional and structural realities. Institutions, rather than functioning to serve and edify human life in the world, have become distorted, usurping, dominating, and even demonic in character and function. For example, economic institutions act to make profit, accumulate wealth, and exploit the poor, workers, and consumers, while ravaging the environment instead of providing for the equitable distribution of goods and services. Political institutions become the domain of the ruling classes and parties, seek to consolidate and expand their power and control, demand conformity and acquiescence, and easily become idolatrous in their totalitarian pretensions instead of serving as forums for dialogue and participatory decision making over questions of public justice and welfare. Educational institutions function to propagandize and socialize to prescribed social roles, grant status and credentials, and prostitute themselves to the purposes of wealth and power instead of serving as centers of learning and maturation.

The frequent observation of sociology that institutions, structures, bureaucracies, and so on are more than the sum of the individuals who make them up and that they often seem to have a life of their own is confirmed by the biblical insights. After years of neglect, the biblical theology of the "principalities and powers" or, simply, "the powers" is being recovered. This discussion regarding "the powers" has been greatly aided by the biblical investigations of H. Berkhof (*Christ and the Powers*), William Stringfellow (*An Ethic for Christians and Other Aliens in a Strange Land*), John Howard Yoder (*Politics of Jesus*), and in the work of Jacques Ellul.

Berkhof enumerates many contemporary realities that fall under the New Testament labels of "powers," "principalities," "authorities," "elements," "spirits," "gods," "demons," "dominions," and "thrones." He names the state, class, race, politics, social struggle, public opinion, accepted morality, human tradition, national interest, religious and ethical rules, the judicial system, ideas, ideologies, and codes of moral life. Stringfellow says the powers are legion and names all institutions, all ideologies, all images, all movements, all causes, all corporations, all bureaucracies, all traditions, all methods, all routines, all conglomerates, all races, all nations, and all idols.

Yoder attempts to categorize the powers as religious structures, intellectual structures (*ologies* and *isms*), moral structures (codes and customs), and political structures (the tyrant, the market, the school, the courts, race, and nation). It is all of these various and many structures, institutions, and corporate realities that the New Testament speaks of as "powers."

Though most of the New Testament references to the powers speak of their fallenness, they were created by God and were, therefore, originally part of the good creation (Col. 1:15–17). Their creation by God also gives them their "creaturely" character, neither made by human hands, nor simply made up from a composite of human creatures and, therefore, not easily subject to human control and guidance, which is the common illusion. The powers were created through Christ and were made to be instruments of God's love in holding human life and society together, preserving it, serving it, ordering it, acting as bonds between God's love and human experience. Their created role was positive, reflecting God's creative love and will.

However, we do not know the powers in their intended and created role. We know them in their dominion over us. The structures of the world which were intended to be our servants have instead become our masters and our oppressors. All this is a consequence of the fall in which the powers also participate. It is not only men and women who have turned in rebellion against God, but also the powers who now seek to separate us from the love of God (Rom. 8:38). No longer instruments of God's love, they are in diametric opposition and rebellion to God's will and purposes. In fact, they have made themselves into gods (Gal. 4:8) and demand worship and absolute allegiance as objects of ultimate value and worth. No longer agents that bind God and humanity together, they now separate and divide, standing as barriers between God and his creation and between God's children. William Stringfellow refers to the fall of the powers as the inversion or reversal of dominion in which the very structures created for the service and enhancement of human life and society now exercise dominion and have captured human beings in *their* service. These powers have become idolatrous in claiming to provide ultimate meaning and truth, in demanding loyalty as if they were the gods of history, and in estranging us from true meaning and from life itself. Their crucial but modest created purpose has been rejected for more totalitarian pretensions, and they have enslaved humanity and history.

Though the powers are fallen and rebellious, they are still used in God's sovereignty to preserve the world from disintegration. They may even be used for God's purposes, sometimes in spite of themselves, sometimes in competition with one another, sometimes in other ways. They still can provide a framework that keeps the world from sinking into chaos. The Apostle Paul tells us that Christ's followers are those who formerly lived under the rule of the powers of the world but were freed from their tyranny when they came to know God in Jesus Christ. Redeemed by Christ, they now trust solely in God and are no longer subservient to the powers of the world (Gal. 4:1–11). In their alienation from God, people come to depend upon the powers and become lost without the structure they provide for the survival of human life and society. This is God's providential care. Though the powers can sometimes be seen as holding life together in a world that doesn't know Christ's liberation, and thus can have some positive function in contrast to complete chaos, the New Testament describes the life lived under the powers as *slavery*, a life of domination that is hardly worthy of the name *life* in comparison with life which is the gift of God in Jesus Christ.

Christ and the Powers

The crucifixion and resurrection of Christ reveal most clearly the true nature of the powers of the world in their enmity to God and, at the same time, bring about the end of their domination of human life in the most decisive defeat in history. The preeminent thing the apostle Paul has to say about the powers is that their sovereignty and dominion has been broken in the work of Christ.

And you, who were dead in trespasses and the uncircumcision of your flesh, God made alive together with him, having forgiven us all our trespasses, having canceled the bond which stood against us with its legal demands; this he set aside, nailing it to the cross. He disarmed the principalities and powers and made a public example of them, triumphing over them in him (Col. 2:13–15, RSV).

For Paul, salvation in Christ is not important merely in relation to personal sin but is especially meaningful as liberation from slavery to the powers of the world.

By living so freely and humanly in the midst of the fallen powers and a captive humanity, Christ shatters the myth and illusion of the absolute authority of the powers. The deceptive illusion that their dominion and ultimate value is at the center of history is the chief weapon of the rebellious powers but was rendered impotent by Christ's demonstration of his own freedom in relation to them. He treated them for what they were rather than for what they claimed to be in their idolatrous self-glorification. Christ's demonstration of true freedom and genuine humanity against the powers of the world led him, as such a life will do, to a cross. Christ's moral independence, his freedom from the slavery of the powers, rebuked and provoked them. He challenged their claim and rule and, not even to save his own life, would he submit to their idolatrous pretensions and slavery. The appearance of one so genuinely free and authentically human so exposed and threatened the fallen powers of the world that they acted in collusion to kill him. The cross is a sign of that freedom where death is swallowed up in victory. Christ's resurrection from the dead vindicates his manner of life and death, seals his victory, and provides the ground for others to live freely and humanly in the midst of the powers by their "being in Christ." Berkhof summarizes this best in *Christ and the Powers*:

By the cross (which must always, here as elsewhere, be seen as a unit with the resurrection) Christ abolished the slavery which, as a result of sin, lay over our existence as a menace and an accusation. On the cross He "disarmed" the Powers, "made a public example of them and thereby triumphed over them." Paul uses three different verbs to express more adequately what happened to the Powers at the cross.

He "made a public example of them." It is precisely in the crucifixion that the true nature of the Powers has come to light. Previously they were accepted as the most basic and ultimate realities, as the gods of the world. Never had it been perceived, nor could it have been perceived, that this belief was founded on deception. Now that the true God appears on earth in Christ, it becomes apparent that the Powers are inimical to Him, acting not as His instrument but as His adversaries. The scribes, representatives of the Jewish law, far from receiving gratefully Him who came in the name of the God of the law, crucified Him in the name of the law. The priests, servants of His temple, crucified Him in the name of the temple. The Pharisees, personifying piety, crucified Him in the name of piety. Pilate, representing Roman justice and law, shows what these are worth when called upon to do justice to the Truth Himself. Obviously, "none of the rulers of this age," who let themselves be worshipped as divinities, understood God's wisdom, "for had they known, they would not have crucified the Lord of glory" (I Corinthians 2:8). Now they are unmasked as false gods by their encounter with Very God; they are made a public spectacle.

Thus Christ has "triumphed over them." The unmasking is actually already their defeat. Yet this is only visible to men when they know that God Himself had appeared on earth in Christ. Therefore we must think of the resurrection as well as of the cross. The resurrection manifests what was already accomplished at the cross: that in Christ God has challenged the Powers, has penetrated into their territory, and has displayed that He is stronger than they.

The concrete evidence of this triumph is that at the cross Christ has "disarmed" the Powers. The weapon from which they heretofore derived their strength is struck out of their hands. This weapon was the power of illusion, their ability to convince men that they were the divine regents of the world, ultimate certainty and ultimate direction, ultimate happiness and the ultimate duty for small, dependent humanity. Since Christ we know that this is illusion. We are called to a higher destiny; we have higher orders to follow and we stand under a greater protector. No powers can separate us from God's love in Christ. Unmasked, revealed in their true nature, they have lost their mighty grip on men. The cross has disarmed them; wherever it is preached, the unmasking and the disarming of the Powers takes place (pp. 30–31).

If the life, death, and resurrection of Christ mean victory over the powers, then this must be the witness and proclamation of the church of Jesus Christ. The church is that new force in history, called into being "so that the manifold wisdom of God should henceforth be made known by means of the church to the principalities and powers in heavenly places, according to the eternal purpose which he set in Jesus Christ our Lord" (Eph. 3:10, 11, RSV). The very existence of a church made up of Jews and Gentiles, formerly walking "according to the powers of the world" and at enmity with one another, now living together in the love and fellowship of Christ is, itself, a sign to the powers that their dominion has been broken. The very presence of a body of people who exercise their moral independence is the most aggressive challenge to the authority and rule of the powers. The church must first show, in its own shared life, that the unbroken dominion of the powers has ended. Without a visible and concrete demonstration of independence, all the church's outward attacks upon the institutions of the world will be doomed to failure. Berkhof, again, comments:

All resistance and every attack against the gods of this age will be unfruitful, unless the church herself is resistance and attack, unless she demonstrates in her life and fellowship how men can live freed from the Powers. We can only preach the manifold wisdom of God to Mammon if our life displays that we are joyfully freed from his clutches. To reject nationalism we must begin by no longer recognizing in our own bosoms any difference between peoples. We shall only resist social injustice and the disintegration of community if justice and mercy prevail in our own common life and social differences have lost their power to divide. Clairvoyant and warning words and deeds aimed at state or nation are meaningful only in so far as they spring from a church whose inner life is itself her proclamation of God's manifold wisdom to the "powers in the air" (*Christ and the Powers*, pp. 42–43).

Yoder claims that the "otherness of the church" is rooted not in weakness but in the strength that comes from noncomformity. The strength of the church "consists in her being a herald of liberation and not a community of slaves." The church, "created by the cross and not by the sword," resists the temptations and seductions of the powers and "by her existence she demonstrates that their rebellion has been vanquished." If the church preaches a liberation and reconciliation to the world that it has not experienced in its own life, its proclamations will be without integrity or power.

Christ has unmasked, exposed, and disarmed the powers of the world. Their unchallenged, unbroken dominion has been ended in his cross and resurrection. His victory guarantees that the powers will be "dethroned" altogether, even the power of death itself (1 Cor. 15), when again he acts and the kingdoms of this world become the kingdoms of our Lord. We now live in the "already" and the "not yet" of the kingdom of God, the tension which fills the New Testament.

The biblical witness presents a sharp contrast between "this world," dominated by the principalities and powers, and the in-breaking of the kingdom of God into human history which breaks the uncontested rule and dominion of the powers. The kingdom of God, inaugurated by Christ, is both a coming reality, eagerly anticipated, and a reality already present and in the making here and now. Jesus ushered in this new order by conquering death and bringing new life. The presence of this new order among us and the promise of its coming consummation provide the basis of hope and value for the Christian. Although not yet complete, the kingdom is a present reality, and the Christian community is to be that "new creation" living in the light of the new reality that we have experienced. Christians, then, are people of a new order and are not to walk in darkness but to walk as children of light (Ephesians 5:11). They are not to conform to the powers of the old order but are to be transformed—a people living by different values and standards. Berkhof clarifies: "The Powers are still present; but where Christ is preached and believed in, a limit has been set to their working. This limit is the sign and promise of their defeat. Primarily, this limitation is seen in the continued existence of the church of Christ." The church is a community of those who "see through the deception of the Powers," refuse their idolatrous claims and designs, "shrink" their meaning and value, challenge their authority over people's lives; "their presence is an interrogation; the questioning of the legitimacy of the Powers." The power of He who is in the church is greater than he who is in the world and the final victory is sure. The gift of discernment is given to the church to aid in witnessing to the victory of Christ over the powers of the world in the battle for the hearts and minds of men and women.

Thus, the structural realities that surround us and affect our lives are fallen powers in open rebellion against God in their exercise of oppressive dominion over human life and society. The church demonstrates Christ's victory over the powers by reminding them of their created role as servants, rebuking them in their idolatrous role as masters, and resisting them in their totalitarian claims and purposes.

Stringfellow points out that the hostility of the powers to human life expresses a subservience and worship to the power of death, which is the preeminent moral reality and consequence of the world's fallen condition. The Word of God is the bearer of life, and the powers are fallen creatures who worship death and are the very instruments of death. Hence, the conflict in the world and the meaning of the battle between the people of God and the powers of the world is one of life against death.

Both Berkhof and Stringfellow describe the weapons and strategies of the powers in their rebellious rule: "propaganda, terror, the artificial ideologizing of all of life, the denial of truth, doublespeak and overtalk, secrecy and boasts of expertise, surveillance and harassment, exaggeration and deception, cursing and conjuring, usurpation and absorption, division and demoralization, etc." Language itself is distorted, inverted, manipulated, and rendered meaningless by, what Stringfellow calls, the violence of Babel—"such profusion of speech and sound that comprehension is impaired, nonsense, sophistry, jargon, noise, incoherence, a chaos of voices and tongues, falsehood, blasphemy." Contemporary examples of all these tactics and characteristics are frighteningly apparent.

The church witness to the victory of Christ consists in creating new patterns of life free from the rule of the powers; acting to neutralize, relativize, demythologize, de-ideologize, and debunk the powers; reducing their claims, scope, territory, authority, and power; taking them only as modest, limited, purely instrumental agents of service and submission to human life. Paul reminds us that we are at war with the powers, not in a state of peaceful coexistence, detente, or cease-fire. Christ has invaded their territory and domain, and we are his agents and representatives. Paul describes our struggle with the fallen powers as spiritual warfare.

For we do not have to wrestle against flesh and blood, but against principalities and powers, against the world rulers of this darkness, against evil spirits in heavenly places (Eph. 6:12, RSV).

We must be prepared to wage this warfare seriously and be armed with the "full armor of God." The weapons Paul names are truth, righteousness, prayer in the Spirit, the gospel of peace, faith, salvation, and the Word of God. These are given so that we might "be strong in the Lord and in the strength of his might . . . stand firm against the schemes of the devil . . . be able to resist in the evil day, and having done everything, to stand firm" (Eph. 6:10–13). We are not here asked to defeat the powers. That is the work of Christ which he has already done and will continue to do. Our task is to be witnesses and signs of Christ's victory by simply standing firmly in our faith and belief against the seduction and slavery of the powers.

Worship and Politics

When the powers of the world demand unconditional allegiance and obedience that assumes human beings should assign them ultimate value, then the worship of God and the assigning of ultimate value to God's kingdom becomes a radical act, a political threat. In fact, worship is where the vitality of the life of the Christian community is most clearly manifest and where the claims and purposes of the idolatrous powers are most clearly threatened. This is contrary to the political "use" and, therefore, abuse of worship which is so common to ideological religion. Rather, it is the simple, joyous, purely offered worship and praise of God who *alone* is the source, author, and giver of life that is the single greatest threat to the powers which worship and serve death. Biblically understood, the worship of God is to be the definition of our lives. Worship is not to be conceived as mere ritual and ceremony apart from ethics, politics, and other parts of life. Instead, worship and praise become the *style of life* for the gathered community living in faithful obedience to the Word of God in the midst of the blasphemy of the fallen powers.

The Christian community must always be asking which of the powers are now most aggressively seeking to bring human life under their control. Discernment is the spiritual gift employed to understand where and how a particular power is on the offensive in the effort to impose conformity and slavery upon the lives of men and women. For us, the modern state is the great power, the great seducer, the great captor and destroyer of human life, the great master of humanity and history in its totalitarian claims and designs. The state as a power or principality has subsumed and subordinated even the other powers of nation, tradition, racial and ethnic cultures, common and constitutional law, local community institutions and groupings, the media, information, education, religion, the professions, movements and causes, the economic system—other principalities which would rival and compete with the state and, perhaps, inadvertently limit its power in benefit of human life. The fusion of the economic principalities and the political principalities into the centralized state is especially significant. The merging of the economic and political functions in the state is no less true of the large capitalist nation-states where the ruling class and their corporations predominate than of the large Communist states where the party and its bureaucracies rule. Most contemporary political controversy takes the "necessity" of the modern centralized state as an accepted premise and starting point and proposes changes and restructuring only within that framework, rather than questioning the legitimacy of the modern nation-state itself and beginning to seek alternatives to it. Thus, most social criticism is conformist and decidedly not radical in merely posing different ideological versions of the same thing.

One of the clearest demonstrations of the extraordinary and pervasive power of the modern state is the frightening instances of so many in the churches actually becoming defenders and apologists of the state's demands for absolute allegiance and obedience. Distorted appeals are made to Romans 13, for example, as if Paul was there instructing uncritical allegiance and unconditional obedience to the dictates of the governing powers, rather than teaching that civil authority, like the other powers and principalities, was created by God to be a servant for the good of human life, preventing chaos and disintegration, promoting good and restraining evil. The New Testament is filled with the tension between this legitimate function of political authority and the state becoming an oppressor in its idolatrous self-glorification and totalitarian behavior which is a terror to good, an incarnation of the evil it is meant to restrain, and the purveyor of the chaos and destruction it is meant to guard against. This demonic potential and character is in every state as a consequence of the fall and the rebellion of the principalities and powers. Thus, the Christian relationship to the state is conditional, critical, vigilant, wary, and always subject to a greater and higher allegiance to the will and purpose of God. Paul's own encounters with the civil authorities in the Book of Acts suggest that what he meant in Romans 13 by *submission* clearly was not a passive acceptance of whatever the state does or desires. The various occurrences of the word *submis-*

sion in the New Testament suggest reciprocity and a proper recognition of the other's standing or place in the creative intentions of God. In reference to the state, submission never means an uncritical, unconditional kind of blind obedience and acceptance and, in certain circumstances, will not include obedience at all but rather a conscientious disobedience when obedience would require disobedience to God. Similarly, to "honor" the civil authorities means to take their vocations seriously—usually more seriously than they take them themselves—as "ministers" and servants of human life in society. It is the vocation of the office more than the occupant which is honored. Honoring the office holder does not exclude critical words of rebuke and correction but will require them when sight is lost of the created purpose of the office. This is what Paul did at Philippi in Acts 16. Jesus rebuked Herod as a "fox" in Luke 13:32. Acts 17 suggests that to proclaim Jesus as Lord was a political threat to the civil authorities. Peter also spoke of proper submission to civil authority but had no problems standing before them in Jerusalem and saying, "We must obey God rather than men" (Acts 5:29, rsv). "Rendering unto Caesar the things that are Caesar's" does not mean giving Caesar everything he asks, and the arbiter of what belongs to Caesar is not Caesar but God to whom we are to render our lives and our obedience.

Paul also shows an awareness of the governing authorities as agents of Satan, doing his "hindering" work (1 Thess. 2:18 as referring to Acts 17). The New Testament recognizes civil authority as created and ordered by God to protect human life from chaos and, at the same time, speaks of the demonic possibilities and character of the fallen state. The paradox and the tension of being both minister of God and instrument of Satan is fundamental to an understanding of the state in the New Testament. These contradictory assertions refer to the state as a principality in both its created service and fallen rebellion. In either case, and in both, the state is nothing absolute, nothing final, nothing ultimate, nothing that bears the true meaning of human life and human history.

The paradoxical stance to the state of the early Christians is dramatically illustrated in the contrast between Romans 13 and Revelation 13 where John the Apostle describes the state as the special incarnation of the powers of evil on earth and a tangible embodiment of Satanic and demonic power in his day. The Roman state is described by John as a "beast from the abyss" empowered by the dragon Satan and endowed with the full powers of the Devil for his work in the world (Rev. 13:1, 2; 17:7–18; 12:9). The beast of Revelation is a parable, an archetype of the triumph of the demonic in any and all nation-states (also note temptation narratives where the kingdoms of this world are in Satan's power to give to Christ).

The great persecutions of the Roman emperors Nero and Domitian began in about A.D. 64, after Paul's Epistle to the Romans written in about A.D. 57, when there was relative calm throughout the provinces. Revelation was not written until the last decade of the first century, at the end of Domitian's reign, when Rome had reached a peak of power and moral brutality. The empire's enormous wealth and luxurious affluence existed in stark contrast to the extreme poverty of the masses (Rev. 18:11–16 and 6:5, 6). Rome's power, corrupting influence, and rampant nationalism of Pax Romana had been experienced throughout the world (Rev. 18:3). Domitian (A.D. 81–96) demanded emperor worship as a test of loyalty. His persecutions were some of the most intense history has known, and Christians bore the brunt of his wrath for stubbornly believing that another should be worshiped instead of the emperor. John wrote the Book of Revelation while a political prisoner on the island of Patmos, a Roman penal settlement in the Aegean Sea. The "Revelation of John" is one of the most political pieces of literature in all of the Bible. It is a political-religious manifesto against the Roman Empire, a Christian tract against the brutal inequities, arrogant injustice, and blasphemous nationalism of the world's most powerful state. Thus, according as the state remains within its proper limits or transgresses them, judged in each situation or circumstance, the Christian community will treat it as a servant of God or as an instrument of the Devil. The Bible sees an inevitable drift toward the demonic inherent in the state which always and irresistibly demands for itself more than it should, indeed, by demanding what is God's alone.

The organic connections between worship and politics are dramatically shown in the Book of the Revelation. A deep and pervasive sense of worship and praise of God fills the entire book and reaches a peak in chapters 17–19 where the fall of Babylon (the city of death which is a parable for Rome and other powerful states where the demonic resides) occasions a great celebration in heaven, "Fallen, fallen is Babylon the great!" The destruction of the powerful and wealthy city is a sign of salvation in the world, a demonstration of God's sovereignty and power over the nations (Rev. 19:1–6). Only those who profited from Babylon's wealth and power mourn her destruction while those who have "come out of her" and disentangled themselves from her corruption rejoice with the heavenly hosts (Rev. 18:4–19). Outbursts of hallelujah ring out from heaven over the destruction of Rome and the great victory which gives glory to God. "Hallelujah! For the Lord our God, the Almighty, is King."

John consistently applies titles to God that are normally reserved for the emperor, "Lord God," "King," and so on, assigning to God the ultimate value, worth, and worship which the emperor retained exclusively for himself. In the first century, "religious" and "political" affirmations were not neatly separated, and religious assertions such as "Jesus is King" or "Yahweh is Lord God" had deep political meaning that provoked the civil authorities. To say that Jesus is Lord was to register a public protest and declare that Caesar was not Lord. It was to make a political as well as a theological affirmation. Proper worship, in this context, had deep political consequences as it would in our context if worship were properly understood.

The charges brought against Jesus were of a political character. He was accused of blasphemy and sedition against Caesar. He was "misleading our nation and forbidding to pay taxes to Caesar and saying that he, himself, is Christ, a king" (Luke 23:2). The same political implications were evident in his opposition, "We have no king but Caesar" (John 19:15). His disciples were also accused, "They all act contrary to the decrees of Caesar, saying that there is another king, Jesus" (Acts 17:7). The political implications of the Lord's Prayer, "Thy kingdom come," are yet to be widely recognized. In the midst of the idolatrous claims of the Roman state and the violent persecution of all who would not conform to the imperial cult, John exclaimed, "Worthy art Thou alone," "Worthy is the Lamb that was slain to receive power, and riches, and wisdom, and strength, and honor, and glory, and blessing."

When Christians defied the absolute authority of the state by worshiping another "king," they were a disruptive political threat. The early believers were imprisoned and killed simply because they worshiped God as Lord and Christ as King and because their lives testified to their worship. Perhaps there are so few Christians in jail in America because we have forgotten how to worship.

4. The Powerful and the Powerless

The Division of the World

The divisions in the world today are less along the lines of ideology than they are along the lines of powerful and powerless, rich and poor, strong and weak, those who benefit and those who are victimized. The scenario of our times is a growing conflict generated by the radical disparity between the rich and poor of the world. The stark contrasts are between rich and poor nations, rich and poor classes. In the arenas where the struggles for social justice are occurring, increasingly, the central questions concern the need for fundamental redistribution of wealth and power on a global scale.

The growing détente between the United States and its principal cold war adversaries, the Soviet Union and China, demonstrate that the divisions in the world today have little to do with ideology and everything to do with the thirst for wealth and power which has historically been the primary motivation and driving force behind the behavior of the dominant nation-states. The dramatic struggle between East and West is being replaced by the conflict of interest between the rich nations of the northern hemisphere and the poor nations of the southern hemisphere. Containment and ideological competition are being replaced with trade, deals, sales, and cooperation for shared commercial and political purposes.

When Russian and Chinese leaders held summit meetings with the United States, at the height of American bombing of North Vietnamese cities and population centers, it became clear to the rest of the world that the Communist giants were willing to sacrifice the Vietnamese people for a piece of the action in a new partnership of superpowers to dominate the world. Scenes of American leaders being wined and dined by the Russian and Chinese heads of state have generated great fear among the poor of the world and show that the desire for wealth and power is still a greater motivating factor than ideology. American business streams into the Soviet Union, new arrangements and agreements are announced with increasing regularity, and American soft drinks become the favorite of the affluent everywhere. As a final bit of irony, the Chase Manhattan Bank has opened a branch at 1 Karl Marx Square in Moscow and has a correspondent relationship with the Bank of China.

The violent rhetoric of the cold war confrontation has subsided as the huge capitalist and socialist bureaucracies find they have much in common with one another as world powers. A shared desire for economic and military domination has even resulted in growing structural and political similarities among the world's most powerful nations. This is true in industry and commerce, in government, in the control of the flow of information, in the silencing of dissent, and in the eroding of basic civil and human rights. These nations share common imperial interests and behavior in their relationships to other countries. When the Soviet Union rolled its tanks into the streets of Prague and crushed the stirrings of independence in Dubcek's Czechoslovakia, the Soviets claimed an inherent right to prevent a country from slipping out of their orbit. That same doctrine operates at the heart of American foreign policy as has been so brutally demonstrated in Vietnam and elsewhere in the Third World. When an insurgent social movement or new government threatens to take a nation out of the United States' economic, political, and military orbit, the American government's often-claimed commitment to self-determination for other countries quickly shows itself to be without substance. When American policymakers feel business, diplomatic, or strategic interests to be threatened by a development in another country, the United States takes the right to conspire unilaterally and act against that threat through economic reprisal and strangulation, political subversion, assassination, paramilitary or military operations. The same tactics are used in aggressively subverting "unfavorable" regimes and in creating circumstances in which American economic and political power is protected and promoted. Both American and Soviet powers have acted to create and maintain client regimes in other countries that exercise control through means of repression, terror, and torture. A totalitarian spirit fuels the engines of both Wall Street and the Kremlin.

The community of interest among the powerful nation-states is creating an international oligopoly of world power. In such a stable and repressive world order, the superpowers find they have more similarities than differences, agree to reduce and marginalize their conflicts even if retaining some of the illusive and superficial rhetoric of ideological conflict, divide the world into market shares or spheres of influence, and exact incredible profits by virtue of their unprecedented degree of dominance and control over the rest of the world. Using the lofty rhetoric and vague ideology of their "global responsibilities" (for example, great power brings great responsibility for global leadership, and so on), they, in reality, strive to create an integrated world system ordered to benefit the material welfare of the large industrial nations. One fact from all of this remains clear: the position of the poor and powerless is further diminished.

Thus, ideological concerns are quickly dropped as the superpowers realize their own self-interest in cooperating in a new alliance of world power conceived at the expense of the world's poor and oppressed majority. This coldly calculated arrangement should hold up provided none of the major powers gets more selfish and pushy than it ought to with its new "business partners." Though all the wealthy and powerful nations are deeply implicated in this alliance against the poor and powerless, the clear leader of this oppressive world order is the United States. American policy has become dominated by the vested interests of an increasingly concentrated corporate power structure which seeks greater control, profit, and power throughout the world with a coherent global strategy to help create and stabilize a system of "open societies" where United States economic, political, and military interests can operate more or less freely. This is the real meaning of America's highly touted "structure of peace in the world." The Pax Americana is reminiscent of another "peace" from another time. Arnold Toynbee, the British historian, comments:

America is today the leader of a world-wide anti-revolutionary movement in defense of vested interests. She now stands for what Rome stood for. Rome consistently supported the rich against the poor in all foreign communities that fell under her sway; and since the poor, so far, have always and everywhere been far more numerous than the rich, Rome's policy made for inequality, for injustice, and for the least happiness of the greatest number. America's decision to adopt Rome's role has been deliberate, if I have gauged it right ("America and the World Revolution," quoted in David Horowitz, *Free World Collossus*, p. 15).

The causes of revolutionary war and violence are not primarily due to conspiracies and outside agitation, but are rooted in the economic and political institutions of the United States and the other major powers and in the values and attitudes of the people of the rich nations. Since the early period of American history, the United States has been characterized by a continuous expansionist thrust, first in striving for territorial acquisition and, more recently, in seeking economic and political control and domination. That same expansionist pattern has dominated the history of the other powerful nations of the modern world. The expansionist thrust has always been represented as a noble effort to advance "freedom," "democracy," "civilization," or some other great value around the world. The obvious questions that comes to mind are: Freedom for whom and freedom for what? Who are the chief beneficiaries and who are the victims of these advances in "democracy" and "civilization"? Cloaked in their own self-righteous rhetoric, the powerful nations in history have actually been engaged in self-interested empire building as each has sought to be the number one nation in the world. A rather clear foreign policy designed to expand American profit and power in the world has not been altered by the changing of presidents and has been consistently practiced by both political parties. American leaders have concluded that "national security" comes only in dominating others which has resulted in a society organized for war on a global scale since 1945. We have witnessed the growing militarization of American life and have watched the United States conduct military and paramilitary campaigns around the world. Less visible ways of intervention include the support of dictatorial regimes which protect American interests, the training of local military and police elites in the effective "control" of social revolution and the use of terror and torture, assassination, and economic and political subversion. The American role as leader of the world's vested interests against the poor comes by virtue of its enormous and far-flung commercial interests and its worldwide deployment of military power. This has brought the growth of elaborate networks and systems of espionage and secret political offensives, of expanded research and development in methods of warfare and counterinsurgency, of huge public relations and propaganda campaigns designed for mass persuasion, of the militarization of science, and of the mobilization of the universities, all adding to the arsenal built to protect an empire.

The key concept is control. The leaders of the rich nations believe that domestic prosperity requires continuing economic and military expansion. To assure markets for their products, sources for raw materials, a regular flow of needed commodities, utilization of cheap labor, and opportunities for highly profitable investment, it is considered essential to maintain control or influence in as many countries as possible. The rich nations have sought to create, on a global scale, those conditions and relationships which guarantee the protection and expansion of their economic and political power. By aggressive investment and trade, by maneuvering the weaker nations into dependent relationships, by use of financial arrangements, military agreements, and political alliances with local elites, the rich nations have forged an empire. It is an empire based upon the influence and control of the political economies of the nonindustrial nations rather than upon territorial conquest and is, therefore, "invisible," an empire without boundaries. Webster's *New Collegiate Dictionary* defines imperialism as "the policy, practice, or advocacy of extending the power and domination of a nation especially by direct territorial acquisition or by gaining indirect control over the political and economic life of other areas." The *American Heritage Dictionary* defines imperialism as "the policy of extending a nation's authority by territorial acquisition or by the establishment of economic and political hegemony over other nations."

"We are the number one nation," said President Lyndon Johnson at a crucial point in the Vietnam War, "and we are going to stay the number one nation." There has never been a more honest and accurate definition of the doctrine of national interests as interpreted by American leaders and policymakers. Staying number one is a struggle for permanent victory. It means to pursue the national interest even at the cost of terror, destruction, and death. The United States, being the richest and most powerful nation, becomes, as Martin Luther King charged, "the greatest purveyor of violence in the world." This happens by virtue of the necessity of protecting American wealth and power in the midst of the world's poor and exploited masses. A dependence upon violence, in its many forms, is inherent in being "number one." The public's willingness to acquiesce when the call is sounded to support "the national interest" is crucial. The uncritical acceptance of the myth of "the national interest" and "national security" is essential in keeping the United States the number one nation.

The system of empire is based upon the consumer society. The constant pressure for an expanding GNP and rising standard of living justifies and requires commercial expansion and the use of political and military power to secure expanded openings for American businessmen around the world. Our ever-growing consumer society is thus at odds with world peace. An international economic system that keeps huge sectors of humanity at a subhuman level while permitting the minority to consume most of the world's resources can only result in conflict. Peace is only possible if the poor and weaker nations of the world are willing to accept the present distribution of wealth and power and the rules of the game as laid down by the United States and the other powerful nations. The tandem of multinational corporations and the military and political power of the world's most powerful governments is the instrument being used to achieve the ends of empire and uphold the consumer society which cannot exist without empire.

We are finally coming to understand a discomforting but central fact of reality—the people of the nonindustrialized world are poor *because* we are rich; the poverty and brutalization of the wretched masses is maintained and perpetuated by our systems and institutions and by the way we live our lives. In other words, the oppressive conditions of life in the poor countries, like the causes of poverty and misery in our own land, are neither merely accidental nor because of the failures of the poor. Our throw-away culture of affluence and wasteful consumption fragments and privatizes our lives. Our consumer orientation lulls us into primary concern for ourselves and into a passive acceptance of the suffering of others —horrors committed in our name in Indochina and elsewhere. At home, our consumerism supports corporate interests that exploit the poor, profit from war, and destroy the environment. Peace, justice, and ecological survival are sacrificed for the rewards and pleasures of affluence. Our present standard and style of life can be maintained or expanded only at the cost of the suppression of the poor of the world.

A survey of poverty conducted by the *New York Times* in 1971 summarized its findings as follows: "There are more poor people than ever . . . and more of them than ever are born into malnutrition and disease. Physically and mentally stunted, they live wretchedly foreclosed lives in which the future means little more than tomorrow's struggle to survive. They die young and hopeless" (quoted in *Social Policy*, May/June 1971). Hunger and disease due to hunger are today responsible for two-thirds of the deaths in the world each year. It is estimated that a child born in America today will consume, during a lifetime, twenty times as much as a child born in India and will contribute fifty times as much pollution to the environment. Of every one hundred babies born in the world, forty will die before age six. Another forty risk permanent physical and mental damage because of malnutrition. Only three out of that hundred will get the education and skills they need to perform creative and meaningful work. While those in the rich nations worry about the potential for violence in the rebellion of the poor against the status quo, they fail to recognize the violence inherent in established structures and relationships that inflict injustice and agony by relegating the poor to subhuman conditions of life.

The brutal disparities between rich and poor are clearly seen even in the midst of affluent nations like the United States. We have learned more about the nature of this country, not through presidential press conferences, but through the eyes of the disadvantaged, the black, brown, red, and poor white minorities locked in urban ghettos of human misery, rat-infested tenements, and rural prisons of poverty. Race and sex are still the basis for denying people their basic human rights, and class and color continue to be the primary factors in determining a person's share of justice, education, health, respect, income, and society's goods and services.

All of this is aggravated and intensified by the growing concentration of economic and political power in the hands of a few persons and institutions. Certain people, classes, and institutions possess an enormous and illegitimate amount of power which is exercised for their own benefit and against social justice and especially against the poor. This power is, at root, economic and comes to dominate and corrupt the political process. In the United States, such power is centered in the small number of large corporations which shape the political economy. The decision making of these large corporations is in the hands of the very few and the very rich. To suppose that corporate decisions are subject to the forces of the "free market" or to a meaningful sense of public accountability is to engage in illusion. These multinational corporations have gained great power and are increasingly able to act quite unilaterally in national and international affairs when their interests are involved. American society itself is organized according to the large corporate model, and corporate interests and profits dominate production, distribution, communication, information, education, technology, entertainment, and of course, politics. The dominant institutions of the American social order, including the churches, reflect the structure and values of the large corporation. The university's servitude to the corporate structure and the warfare state is a prime example.

A specter of death dominates the corporate structures, the political institutions, the legal system, the Pentagon, the rule of technology, the labor unions, the social, cultural, and religious bureaucracies, the competing ideologies, and the environment itself. We suffer the reality of fear, the guilt of silence, and the paralysis of conscience. The system is indeed guilty, but we are all implicated to the extent that its values have become our own.

We confront a socio-economic-political system based on the dominance of the few over the many and the affluent life-style of the American people that supports such a system at home and around the world. When rich nations gain wealth and power through exploitation, conflict, suffering, and violence are assured.

John Woolman, an early American Quaker, once said, "May we look upon our treasures, the furniture of our houses, and our garments, and try whether the seeds of war have nourishment in these our possessions" (quoted in *Simplicity* newsletter, Spring 1974).

The prophets spoke of God's anger with the politics of oppressive affluence:

O my people! Your guides lead you astray and confuse the path that you should take. The Lord comes forward to argue his case and stands to judge his people. The Lord opens the indictment against the elders of his people and their officers: You have ravaged the vineyard, and the spoils of the poor are in your houses. It is nothing to you that you crush my people and grind the faces of the poor? This is the very word of the Lord, the Lord of Hosts (Isa. 3:12–15, NEB).

The gospel is clearly biased in favor of the poor and oppressed. There is a biblical mandate to support the cause of the poor against the abuses of wealth and power. In America, to accept the status quo means to support the rich against the poor. We pursue our material comfort at the cost of impoverishing others. In fact, our life-styles and our consumption directly support the suppression of the poor, at home and around the world.

The American empire cannot be resisted merely by political and economic means. Claude Julien, in his book *America's Empire,* says it well:

The struggle for or against the empire is thus not merely a struggle for or against the empire's economic and military structures. It is fundamentally a struggle for or against the type of civilization which America claims to exemplify for humanity. It is a struggle for or against the so-called society of abundance, for or against a consumer society which permits 6 percent of the world's population to absorb half the world's output. This struggle does not occur only between rich and poor countries; it goes on internally in industrialized countries where minorities refuse to kow-tow to the requirements of the consumer society by asserting another system of values, another form of civilization, another concept of the relationships possible between individuals, as well as between rich and poor countries (p. 417).

There could not be a more clear call to the church—that body that is most dynamic when it is most a minority and that lives in radical contradiction to the values of the world by its proclamation and demonstration of a whole new order called the kingdom of God. Will the church that has become so united to the purposes of the state be freed to live in tension and provide a clear vision of the kingdom? Or will its witness continue to be compromised and its proclamation fall on deaf ears? Our churches, by their life-style, social prestige, and relationships are most identified with the elite and power groups of our society rather than with the poor and the oppressed. Our Christian institutions are often dependent on parts of the American establishment which oppress the poor of the earth. To come to terms with the gospel will cost the churches a lot.

One question is whether we are committed to a world order in which the needs for justice and peace are subordinated to the interests of the American establishment. The other question is whether the violence and injustice of a world order of American dominance will only be overturned by the counterviolence of those who are the victims of the American world order. That is a scenario of endless war, endless revolution, endless death and destruction. That consequence is inevitable unless some of those who have benefited from the American world order withdraw their allegiance from it, resist its designs and demands, repudiate its basic assumptions and values, and begin to construct alternatives to it in a way that might provide a new kind of leadership and direction in the wealthy nations. That is a mission of peace, of reconciliation, of evangelism, of prophetic ministry—a mission for the church.

The Church's Identity with the Poor

Questions concerning wealth, poverty, and economic justice take a central place throughout the Bible. The sheer bulk of the biblical teaching about the rich and the poor is overwhelming. The Old Testament is filled with it. Jesus talks more about it than almost any other single issue. The apostles regard the relationship to money and the poor as a primary test of obedience to God. The people of God, both in the Old and New Testaments, are seen as comprising an *economic alternative* to the prevailing assumptions of the world that surrounds them. Contrary to the dominant attitude of our own society, our economic life and standard of living is not a private matter. It is a critical issue of faith and discipleship. Not only is the Bible's teaching on the rich and the poor striking in its quantity, it is uncomfortably plain and clear in its meaning. The Scriptures are not neutral on questions of economics. The God of the Bible is clearly and emphatically on the side of the poor, the exploited, and the victimized.

Throughout Scripture is the insistence that a vital relationship to God will evidence itself in an active serving of social and political justice as witness to God's gift of life over against the world's domination by death. The prophets warned that piety, proper religion, and ritual observance are inadequate. They demanded economic and political justice for the poor, the exploited, the oppressed, the defeated, the defenseless, the weak, the alien. Isaiah tells us that the fast in which God delights involves breaking the yoke of oppression, sharing our bread with the hungry, and bringing the homeless poor into our homes (58:5-7). Amos claims that worship and praise are not acceptable to God unless justice rolls down like waters and righteousness like an ever-flowing stream (5:21-24). The coming of Jesus, as we have noted, brings social revolution. The poor, the sick, the outcast, the downtrodden were objects of Christ's compassion. In fact, when questioned if he was the "one to come" from God, Jesus offered proof of his messiahship by his ministry to the concrete needs of the suffering and afflicted (Matt. 11:5). Later on, Jesus warns those who would call his name that they will be judged by how they respond to the hungry, the poor, the naked, the imprisoned, the sick, and the stranger. The parable of the Good Samaritan demonstrates that our responsibility for our neighbor extends to anyone in need and leaps over the human barriers of race and class at personal cost of time, money, and danger. The apostles repeatedly claim that faith without works that demonstrate obedience is dead, that the quality of our love for God is shown in our practical and sacrificial love for our brothers and sisters.

Nowhere in Scripture are the rights of the rich proclaimed, where God is seen as the Savior and defender of the rich and their wealth, where the poor are exhorted to serve the needs of the rich and be poor for the sake of the wealthy. Throughout Scripture, however, the rights of the poor are proclaimed; God is revealed as their Savior, deliverer, and avenger; and the rich are instructed to serve the poor and relinquish their wealth and power for the sake of the poor. Nowhere in Scripture is wealth praised or admired or the rich upheld and exalted over the poor. In many places in the Bible, however, the poor are blessed and uplifted, and the message of God's Word carries with it the hope of justice and liberation for the poor. Riches and the wealth of possessions is seen in the Bible as, at best, a great spiritual danger and, most often, as a sign of sinful disobedience to God. Just because the rich are rich, it will be harder for them to enter into the kingdom than for a camel to pass through the eye of a needle. The gospel is preached to the poor, and the rich are told to sell what they have and give to the poor for the sake of the kingdom.

Jesus knew that money and possessions are not mere peripheral issues but deeply spiritual concerns that are at the core of human experience and, perhaps, reveal more about an individual than any other aspect of a person's life. The danger of riches in the Old Testament is in the misuse of wealth and power in the oppression and exploitation of the poor. The earth and its fullness belong only to God and are given for the life and development of all God's children. The Jewish tradition of the Jubilee Year provides for a periodic redistribution of land and wealth which militated against the accumulation of riches. In the thunderings of the prophets, God was powerfully revealed as the God of the poor and dispossessed, pouring out his wrath upon the rich and powerful whose affluence crushed the poor and powerless.

In the New Testament, the teaching on wealth is intensified, and the possession of wealth is seen as a great spiritual danger. The possession of wealth twists and distorts people's priorities and values and is a crucial obstacle in their sensitivity to God. The New Testament condemns, not just improper attitudes toward wealth, but also the mere possession of undistributed wealth. One of the very first tests of discipleship to Jesus Christ is a radical change in one's relationship to money and the possession of wealth. The demands of mammon are completely irreconcilable with a total commitment to God. Jesus says, "You cannot serve God and mammon." Notice that he does not suggest that you should not; he simply says that you cannot. This is based upon the assumption that the will of God and the demands of mammon are in direct contradiction to each other, and loyalty must be given to one or to the other. If Jesus was so concerned about the danger of money and possessions in a simple agrarian society, how much more do we, living in the most affluent nation the world has ever known, need to break radically with the power and authority of money and possessions in our lives. An affluent church witnesses to its radical dependence upon wealth, not upon God, and has almost nothing to say to the dispossessed majority of the globe.

We need to hear again the words of the New Testament applied with their full force to us.

Woe to you that are rich, for you have received your consolation. Woe to you that are full now, for you shall hunger (Luke 6:24–25, RSV).

It is easier for a camel to go through the eye of a needle than for a rich man to enter the kingdom of God (Matt. 19:24, RSV).

So therefore, whoever of you does not renounce all that he has cannot be my disciple (Luke 14:33, RSV).

Do not lay up for yourselves treasures on earth, . . . but lay up for yourselves treasures in heaven, . . . For where your treasure is, there will your heart be also (Matt. 6:19–21, RSV).

No one can serve two masters; . . . You cannot serve God and mammon (Matt. 6:24, RSV).

Lord, when did we see thee hungry or thirsty or a stranger or naked or sick or in prison, and did not minister to thee? . . . Truly, I say to you, as you did it not to one of the least of these, you did it not to me (Matt. 25:44, 45, RSV).

Other seed fell among thorns and the thorns grew up and choked it, and it yielded no grain. . . . they are those who hear the word, but the cares of the world, and the delight in riches, and the desire for other things, enter in and choke the word, and it proves unfruitful (Mark 4:7, 18–19, RSV).

Take heed, and beware of all covetousness; for a man's life does not consist in the abundance of his possessions (Luke 12:15, RSV).

I do not mean that others should be eased and you burdened, but that as a matter of equality your abundance at the present time should supply their want (2 Cor. 8:13–14, RSV).

Be sure of this, that no immoral or impure man, or one who is covetous (that is, an idolater), has any inheritance in the kingdom of Christ and of God. Let no one deceive you with empty words, for it is because of these things that the wrath of God comes upon the sons of disobedience (Eph. 5:5, 6, RSV).

If we have food and clothing, with these we shall be content. But those who desire to be rich fall into temptation, into a snare, into many senseless and hurtful desires that plunge men into ruin and destruction. For the love of money is the root of all evils (1 Tim. 6:8–10, RSV).

What does it profit, my brethren, if a man says he has faith but has not works? Can his faith save him? If a brother or sister is ill-clad and in lack of daily food, and one of you says to them, "Go in peace, be warmed and filled," without giving them the things needed for the body, what does it profit? So faith by itself, if it has no works, is dead (James 2:14–17, RSV).

By this we know love, that he laid down his life for us; and we ought to lay down our lives for the brethren. But if any one has the world's goods and sees his brother in need, yet closes his heart against him, how does God's love abide in him? (1 John 3:16–17, RSV).

There is such an overwhelming gap between the life-style of the average middle-class American and the rest of the world that we can no longer pretend that we are not the rich. It is the "just comfortable" standard of living in the rich nations that is such a sharp and brutal contrast and contradiction to the lives of the poor of the earth. We must begin to face the harsh reality that everything the Bible says about the rich applies to us. No longer must our words put us on the side of the oppressed and our style of life put us on the side of the oppressors. Our overconsumption is theft from the poor. God did not give the Americans half the world's resources to be good stewards of; rather, the Americans have stolen those goods from the poor. Unless we are willing to stand with the oppressed by first breaking our attachment to wealth and comfort, all our talk of justice is sheer hypocrisy. The stating of principles and good intentions, the denunciations of crying injustices, the endless declarations, will lack any weight or moral authority apart from a deep awareness of our responsibility before God and our hungry neighbors to give up our privileged position of comfort and affluence and invest ourselves in the struggle against all systems and arrangements which serve to reward the rich and punish the poor. Justice demands fundamental redistribution of wealth and power on both personal and institutional levels.

It is well to remember that the mark of sacrificial giving in the

New Testament is not in how much is given but rather, in how much is left over after the giving is finished (Luke 21:1-4). We cannot give sacrificially and still remain wealthy. It is critical that we constantly heed the biblical warning against minimizing the cost of a visible, outward break with the power of money and possessions. An affluent church cannot say, "Gold and silver have I none," but neither can it say, "In the name of Jesus of Nazareth, walk!"

The church is the body of Christ. This dramatic biblical metaphor speaks of the powerful way the work of Christ has united us to him and to each other. It means that Christ is alive and present in the community and is head over the body. It means that the church is called to embody the presence of Christ in the world by obeying his words, reflecting his mind, and continuing his mission in the world by following the manner and style of his life, death, and resurrection. Jesus tells us that he came into the world not to be served but to serve, and so it is with us. Our vocation is to serve men and women in his name. We are called, not to be conquerors, but to be a self-giving body whose leader was crucified on a cross and asks his followers to take up that same cross. We are called, not to accumulate wealth and influence or to strive to manipulate power, but to empty ourselves as he did for the sake of others.

We are called to give a cup of cold water in his name which will mean feeding the hungry, meeting the needs of the homeless and the refugees, supporting the imprisoned, befriending the lonely, standing with the poor and the outcasts, loving the unloved. This means confronting with our lives the institutional and root causes of the wretched condition of the oppressed. The life which Christ gives is meant to be spread about and not hoarded and shut up for the private edification of the believers. The compassion of Christ always resulted in action, and so must ours. John, the apostle, exhorts us:

It is by this that we know what love is: that Christ laid down his life for us. And we in our turn are bound to lay down our lives for our brothers. But if a man has enough to live on, and yet when he sees his brother in need shuts up his heart against him, how can it be said that love for God dwells in him?

My children, love must not be a matter of words or talk; it must be genuine, and show itself in action. This is how we may know that we belong to the realm of truth (1 John 3:16–19, NEB).

The cross of Christ is both the symbol of our atonement and the pattern for our discipleship. Today many who name the name of Christ have removed themselves from human hurt and suffering to places of relative comfort and safety. Many have sought to protect themselves and their families from the poor and wretched masses for whom Christ showed such primary concern. In affluent societies, our approach to social problems is to decrease their visibility. The migration patterns of Christians and their churches have again reflected the dominant social practice. The church's compassionless inactivity stems from being removed and out of touch with the suffering of the poor and exploited. This modern isolation from human hurt is a major obstacle to being faithful to the biblical mandates. How can we open our hearts and lives to those whom we have hardly ever seen, let alone ever known?

The biblical idea of love carries with it the deliberate extension of ourselves to others. The incarnation, the supreme act of God's love, required the intentional plunge of the Lord of Glory into the chaotic, violent, and rebellious human situation at tremendous cost (Phil. 2:6–11). But this act brought the salvation of the world. We cannot profess the name of Jesus without seeking to incarnate his pattern of self-emptying love and servanthood. Again, this is not merely an individual effort but a corporate one undertaken by a body of people who have given themselves over to Christ and his kingdom, to each other, and to serving in the midst of the broken world for whom he died.

To live in radical obedience to Jesus Christ means to be identified with the poor and oppressed. If that is not clear in the New Testament, then nothing is. God entered the human situation as one of the poor and powerless. Jesus Christ gave himself to the outcasts, the forsaken, the despised, and the rejected, and because of that he too became despised and rejected by the world. He became one of them. His gospel was preached to the poor, and the wretched masses flocked to hear him and be healed by him. The poor, the defenseless, the weak, the sick, the vulnerable came to him because they had nowhere else to go. They became his people. He was sent to them to champion their cause, to comfort their spirits, to share their lives, to love them, to be with them. He refused to exercise power and control over them but came among them as a servant. When they tried to make him their king, he withdrew to the hills to pray. Instead, he would simply serve them, show them God's love for them, and ultimately give up his life in their behalf. He would serve them in whatever ways their needs required all for the joy of just being with them and doing God's will among them. If the poor were Christ's people and we are his body, then the poor become our people. If Christ was the servant of the poor, then, among the poor, the church lives as a servant people. Thomas Merton speaks of the meaning of the incarnation:

Into this world, this demented inn, in which there is absolutely no room for Him at all, Christ has come uninvited. But because He cannot be at home in it, because he is out of place in it, his place is with those others for whom there is no room. His place is with those who do not belong, who are rejected by power because they are regarded as weak, those who are discredited, who are denied the status of persons, who are tortured, bombed, and exterminated. With those for whom there is no room, Christ is present in the world. He is mysteriously present in those for whom there seems to be nothing but the world at its worst. . . . It is in these that He hides Himself, for whom there is no room (Raids on the Unspeakable, quoted in The Catholic Worker, December 1973).

The gospel knows nothing of what sociologists call "upward mobility." In fact, the gospel of Jesus Christ calls us to the reverse; the gospel calls us to a downward pilgrimage. Former attachments and securities in the false values of wealth and power are left behind as we are empowered by the Holy Spirit to seek first the kingdom. From an obscure birth in a dirty animal stable to the crucifixion of a poor suffering servant who never had a place to lay his head, the gospel witnesses to God's identification with the poor and powerless. Such a life of identification will bring rejection, abuse, and opposition from the world, and if one becomes too prominent, one might even be crucified. We may measure our obedience to the gospel by the degree of tension and conflict with the world that is present in our lives. If our lives are secure, comfortable, and at home with wealth and power, we belong to the world rather than to Christ. We are to be identified with the poor and victimized because we have been given the heart and mind of Christ. *Metanoia* has taken place, and we are freed to reject the false values of the world for the real values of the kingdom. Obedience to Christ involves relinquishing the power of the world until our lives are cast with the poor, the weak, the exploited, the abandoned, those who have no worldly power. Gordon Cosby, pastor of the Church of the Savior, in Washington, D.C., describes the downward pilgrimage of discipleship.

At the bottom are the poor and impotent, their minds and gifts never developed; they are the dumping ground of human life. They couldn't tell you what the human potential movement is, much less be in the stream of that movement. They are buffeted to and fro because of their helplessness, as those who are helpless are always buffeted to and fro by the powerful. They have no one to protect them, no one to speak for their rights. They are the lonely ones. You'll find them in prisons and in psychiatric hospitals, their children are in the welfare system. They are jobless, hungry, thirsty. Their options are extremely limited. They are not wanted. In their present state they could not possibly build institutions to secure their rights and their privileges, because they have so few. We, in our contempt, look down from our secure vantage point and call them rabble, and riffraff. They, they, they.

Part of the scandal of the gospel is that when you meet the abandoned, crucified Messiah, he grabs you and you belong to him. Wherever you are in privilege and power and status and opportunity, you start the movement down, not up. And you go down and down and down until you are powerless, except for his power; you go down until you find yourself with the riffraff. The evangelists that I listened to in my youth didn't make that clear. But the evangelists in the New Testament make that devastatingly clear. One keeps going down and down until one is identified with the victimized poor wherever they are scattered throughout the earth. Wherever you see them and hear about them, you know that your lot is cast with them, that they are your people.

This downward pilgrimage, again, drives us to community and is meant to take place in the context of a common shared life. The life of the early Christian fellowships, as seen in the Book of Acts and elsewhere in Scripture, presents the Christian life as a common life, the life of a people more than the life of individuals. Here were the ones who had known Jesus, had walked with him, talked with him, listened to him, and lived with him for three years. They had seen him live and die and rise again from the dead. They were eyewitnesses to the gospel. They had both followed him and forsaken him. Their lives had been decisively and irrevocably changed by him. He had set their feet upon a new path, and they would never be the same again. In response to his command, they gathered in an upper room to wait for the promised coming of the Spirit.

At the day of Pentecost, they were all in one place, waiting, when suddenly there came a sound like "a strong driving wind" and "they were all filled with the Holy Spirit." The consequence of the outpouring of the Spirit was a bold and mighty proclamation of the gospel, repentance on the part of many who saw and heard, and the establishment of a *common life* among the believers.

They met constantly to hear the apostles teach, and to share the common life, to break bread, and to pray. A sense of awe was everywhere, and many marvels and signs were brought about through the apostles. All whose faith had drawn them together held everything in common: they would sell their property and possessions and make a general distribution as the need of each required. With one mind they kept up their daily attendance at the temple, and, breaking bread in private houses, shared their meals with unaffected joy, as they praised God and enjoyed the favour of the whole people. And day by day the Lord added to their number those whom he was saving (Acts 2:42–47, NEB).

The coming of the Spirit resulted in a common life springing up among the early believers.

The whole body of believers was united in heart and soul. Not a man
of them claimed any of his own possessions as his own, but everything
was held in common, while the apostles bore witness with great power
to the resurrection of the Lord Jesus. They were all held in high esteem;
for they had never a needy person among them, because all who had
property in land or houses sold it, brought the proceeds of the sale, and
laid the money at the feet of the apostles; it was then distributed to
any who stood in need (Acts 4:32–35, NEB).

The holding of "all things in common" was not merely a futile
experiment nor did this practice end at Jerusalem. Rather, the
common life and sharing are shown throughout the New Testament and became the distinguishing mark of the early church. The
shared common life is a direct contradiction to the ordinary social
value that the possession of money and property carries the in-
alienable right to use and dispose of those assets for one's own
benefit. The doctrine of private property as the right to utilize all
of one's material and other resources for one's own purposes,
desires, and satisfaction is a ruling social axiom. However, this
most basic economic assumption is decidedly not Christian.
Rather, the descriptions of the Christian fellowships in Acts and
elsewhere point to a common use and consumption of resources,
assets, and gifts of the body. The key here is the common use
according to need rather than a particular form or legal status of
common ownership.

The spirit had shattered the normal assumptions of the economic order, and the early believers realized that the way of
Christ militated against the private use and disposition of resources and led to the sharing of all money, property, possessions,
and assets as needs arose in the community. Every gift, blessing,
and material resource would be at the service of the entire community rather than consumed at private discretion and will. Material resources, no less than spiritual gifts, were to be shared and
freely given for the good of the body and not for the personal gain
and advantage of the one who possesses them. A whole new system of distribution had been created in God's new community
with each person in a process of giving and receiving according to

ability and need. The self-giving of the church, as the history of the early church testifies, happens within the body and also spreads out to any and all who are poor and in need. The people of God will always and everywhere follow the will of their God and the example of their Lord in serving the poor and powerless masses of the earth. In its life as a servant people, the church is guided by the Holy Spirit and energized by the love of Christ that has transformed our lives. Jesus Christ is the leader of the new community. In John 17, he prays for the new community.

But now I am coming to thee; and these things I speak in the world, that they may have my joy fulfilled in themselves. I have given them thy word; and the world has hated them because they are not of the world, even as I am not of the world. I do not pray that thou shouldst take them out of the world, but that thou shouldst keep them from the evil one. They are not of the world, even as I am not of the world. Sanctify them in the truth; thy word is truth. As thou did send me into the world, so I have sent them into the world. And for their sake, I consecrate myself, that they may also be consecrated in truth. I do not pray for these only, but also for those who are to believe in me through their word, that they may all be one; even as thou, Father, art in me, and I in thee, that they also may be in us, so that the world may believe that thou hast sent me (John 17:13–21, RSV).

5. The New Community

Alternative Social Reality

The church's greatest problems in confronting sin and death in the world are not merely in forgetting to denounce the world's ills, nor even its inability to make social change effectively. The church's most serious shortcomings stem from its failure to *be* what the church has been called to be, from failing to structure its life and action as that new community created by the work of Christ and empowered by the Holy Spirit to be a new social reality, a living testimony to the presence of the kingdom of God in the world. Thus, the renewal of the church will come not through a recovery of personal experience or straight doctrine, nor through innovative projects of evangelism or social action, nor in creative techniques of liturgical worship, nor in the gift of tongues, nor in new budgets, new buildings, and new members. The renewal of the church in our time will come about through the work of the Spirit in restoring and reconstituting the church as a local community whose common life bears the marks of radical obedience to the lordship of Jesus Christ.

Our churches are now, in most every instance, bearing the marks of a paralyzing conformity to the world that has crippled our life and our witness. We have adopted the structure and values of the large corporation in our organizational patterns. Having become like other institutions and bureaucracies, we employ the same techniques and methods. The ordinary social values are reproduced rather than reversed in the churches, and we have substituted a captive civil religion for the clear proclamation of the Word of God. Throughout Scripture, God speaks strong judgment against the professing community which has conformed to the life and mind of the world around it and is resistant to change. Basic and primary to the task of Christians today is to recover the biblical vision of the church as the people of God—a new social reality in the midst of the life of the world. The biblical metaphors for the people of God—aliens, exiles, pilgrims, sojourners, strangers, salt, light—must be revived and made real again in our everyday experience. If that salt loses its savor, if the light is swallowed up in the darkness, they no longer fulfill their intended purpose and are good for nothing. The church's service and mission in the world is absolutely dependent on its being *different* from the world, being *in* the world but not *of* the world.

Flowing from the call to repentance and discipleship is the invitation to join the new community, the voluntary society, the new peoplehood of those who have begun to experience the salvation of Christ and, together, bear witness to the new life and freedom which Christ brings. This new social reality bears witness to the new order of the kingdom in the midst of a world still dominated by the old order which is passing away.

The New Testament affirms a basic tension between the values and character of the kingdom of God (the new order) and the assumptions and structure of the systems of the world (the old order). Practically, this means a clear recognition, on our part, that the demands of obedient discipleship will bring us into conflict with the ordinary social values and normal patterns of the world systems which continually seek to fashion us in their image and conform us to their molds. The principalities and powers of the world, in their dominance and violence, require a silent and passive church that can be used and manipulated rather than feared for its life-giving power and witness. A serious commitment to follow Christ demands that we resist the efforts of the world to compromise our faith and destroy our witness to the healing and transforming power of the gospel.

We are not left to determine the shape of our discipleship alone.

God has given his people the gift of community. A community of faith and struggle becomes imperative as a center of resistance to the old order and celebration of the new, an environment in which we find the healing of our own brokenness and a sign to the world of the new possibilities of life in Jesus Christ. This is the kind of faith community the New Testament calls the church. It can take different forms in different times and places, but to be the church there must be community present among the believers. The gospel calls us, not only to a new style of life, but to a *new environment* created by Christ to bring about our healing and the healing of the nations.

Christian community must be active, first of all, in creating new awareness of the meaning of our faith and the nature of the world in which we live and seek to bear witness. New awareness of the structures, social values, and historical forces presently operating in the world is essential to the task of discernment. Most critically, new understanding is needed of the nature and demands of the Christian calling and how it relates to responsible participation in the life of the world. Since what we do usually derives from who we believe we are, a primary problem in our churches today is that we simply do not understand who we are as the people of God. We have lost touch with our identity as Christians. Christian community can sharpen that awareness.

Second, Christian community must be a place for the creation of new styles of life based upon a new awareness. It is a place for facilitating the development of new styles of life that begin to free people from the intense pressures and demands of the present forms and patterns of the world. Such a work enables people to see their lives changed in fundamental ways and allows them to participate in a corporate witness to the presence of Christ in the world. The fellowship of believers becomes the first fruits of the kingdom, a sort of pilot project of a whole new order of things.

Third, Christian community can begin to evoke creative responses to the world that arise from a new awareness and a new life-style. These responses bear witness to the faith and life of the community and become signs that point to the possibility of revolutionary change. These responses must confront the idolatries and powers of the world system that seek to stamp people with their image in an assault upon human life and values. That confrontation can open up new possibilities for change and the construction of alternatives. To create new awareness, to generate new styles of life, to evoke creative responses, it is absolutely essential that a community be characterized by a serious study of the Bible, a careful examination of the social, economic, political, and historical forces of our times, and a radical dependence upon prayer and the guidance of the Holy Spirit.

The making of community is essentially a revolutionary act. It is revolutionary because it proposes to detach men and women from their dependence upon the dominant institutions, powers, and idolatries of the world system and creates an alternative corporate reality based upon deviant social values, which challenges the hold of the world system over the lives of people. The most politically responsible undertaking for men and women of faith is to rebuild the church which, when biblically understood, is a spiritual task that creates a revolutionary situation. Repentance and redirection are possible for people only when they are presented with an alternative. It is crucial that we not merely speak of alternatives but, rather, begin to live and be those alternatives. Most importantly, the church is to be a sign of Christ's presence in the world rather than an ecclesiastical reproduction of the twisted values of a technocratic society. The church's life must show practical and demonstrative manifestations of the meaning of Christ that a broken world cannot fail to recognize.

Our time is one of large-scale and concentrated power, of giant corporate institutions whose influence is nearly all pervasive. We have grown to depend upon large corporations and state bureaucracies for our basic needs and, to a frightening extent, have allowed these institutions to decide for us how we will live. In many ways, their values have become our own. Large institutions of concentrated power and influence consciously seek to bring people's lives into conformity with their will and purposes. Large-scale technology, huge amounts of private capital, and a growing economic and political centralization place tremendous power in the hands of a few people. Most of our decisions are made for us by the institutions to whose presence and authority we have all become so accustomed. Power elites, whether they be directors of corporate capitalism or of central state bureaucracies, act to control and dominate, removing the decision-making process from the people who are affected by the decisions. The predominance of these giant institutions is unprecedented and is supreme in production, distribution, and control of the economic process, in the political arena of public policy both domestic and foreign, in information, advertising, and the mass media, in education and cultural activities, in labor and the various professions, in the legal and judicial process, in religion. The population has forfeited decision making to the all-powerful institutions in exchange for a "prepackaged" life of comfort, security, convenience. The public has become consumed with "needs" created by the controlling institutions and then fulfilled in ways to make the population into a dependent, servile, and docile mass society.

These economic and political structures that dominate the world suppress masses of humanity while they keep the rest in mindless conformity. They hurt and destroy more people than the worst of wars and do it all in the name of business as usual, through the natural, regular, and legal operations of the systems of the world. These structures have one primary aim—their own self-interest and perpetuation. Human costs and considerations have little or no place in the decisions made by the ruling principalities and powers.

These dominant institutions control not only socioeconomic and political systems but also shape cultural patterns and engineer the very personal values of the population. This is because the vast majority of the people depends upon them for their very livelihood and security and cannot afford to fall out of favor with them. These institutions have developed sophisticated and intimidating methods of reward, punishment, and threat that can easily be enforced. In such a situation, the values and priorities of the institutions become the values and priorities of the people.

The greatest source of power these institutions have is not merely political or economic but is in the spiritual hold they have over people's lives. The very people who are, in a real sense, controlled by an institution become the chief source of support for the institution's perpetuation. People are turned into loyal employees, frenzied consumers, and obedient citizens. In the biblical scheme of things, this is exactly how sin and death exercise their spiritual authority over people's lives.

For we are not contending against flesh and blood, but against the principalities, against the powers, against the world rulers of this present darkness, against the spiritual hosts of wickedness in the heavenly place (Eph. 6:12, rsv).

The obvious implication of all this is that the power of the dominant structures of the world cannot be fought with political and economic means alone. In fact, political and economic efforts and alternatives against these powerful institutions will be futile and easily co-opted if they are not deeply rooted and founded upon the more profound biblical reality which sees us as engaged in "spiritual warfare" with these principalities and powers of the present world. We cannot restrict our fight against the principalities and powers to the same weapons that they have at their disposal, the weapons which they have a clear monopoly over, the weapons of the world system which are the natural sources of their power. To do so is to insure our defeat or is to seek a "victory" which is, in reality, merely another victory for the world system and another defeat for human life and freedom. Fundamental change will not take place through the weapons of the world nor within the present structure of the systems of the world. Rather, we must wage "spiritual warfare" with the principalities and powers, employing weapons that are at *our* disposal, weapons that are the natural sources of *our* power as the people of God (Eph. 6:11–20). We employ the weapons of "truth," "righteousness," "faith," "salvation," "the gospel of peace," "prayer," "the Spirit," "perseverance," "intercession," and the "Word of God." In so doing, we "find strength in the Lord, in his mighty power" and are enabled "to stand firm against the devices of the devil" and to "resist" and "stand our ground when things are at their worst, to complete every task and still to stand."

The spiritual hold of the dominant institutions of the world system over people's lives must be broken. Refusal to give the demanded allegiance, withdrawal of loyalty and support, and ending conformity to their purposes is the greatest threat to the principalities and powers. Without people's subservience and passive obedience, the powers of the world find their spiritual hold over people's lives rendered impotent. The treatment of Jesus at the hands of the authorities and the official paranoia over every radical dissenter in history demonstrates the deep fear of the principalities and powers when the legitimacy of their authority is challenged and a confrontation with the truth exposes the idolatrous character of their power.

The gospel of salvation in Christ must be addressed to people's need to be freed from the idolatrous power and domination of the strongest institutions of the world system. The action of God in changing people's lives and enabling them to live in a different way is at the heart of the gospel message. Throughout the Bible, the path of obedience to God is a communal pilgrimage, not merely an individual trek. Corporate strength and power cannot be countered through individual effort alone but must be resisted with *another form* of corporate power with a different set of values and assumptions. The dominance and control of the large institutions of the present system must and can be resisted with the new corporate strength that comes from a body of believers who share their lives together, support one another, take liability and responsibility for one another, hold one another accountable to a common commitment, reinforce a set of values that is deviant from the larger society, and are empowered by the Holy Spirit.

The greatest influence on a person's life will be that institution or set of institutions on which the person feels most dependent for survival and support. As long as most Christians are more dependent upon the powers and principalities of the world for their survival and security than they are upon the Christian community, the church cannot do anything other than conform to the world. We must see through biblical eyes that our lives and our very spiritual survival, personally, economically and politically, must be centered in the Christian community. The community of the local church must become the most important and central corporate reality of our lives, the daily environment out of which our lives are lived, the fellowship of people that sustains and supports us. The church must represent a body of people who have committed their lives to one another in Christ, a communion of faith and trust in which everything is shared, a place where our lives and society are seen through the eyes of biblical faith, a corporate sign of the transforming power of the gospel of the kingdom in the world.

The church is called to relate to the world as a new community of people who are being transformed by Christ. This means that, first of all and at the basis of everything we do, we must seek to become a kingdom-conscious body of people who, by their very existence and presence, call into question the values, assumptions, and very structure of their world and free people to live in alternative ways. The churches must be reevangelized to this biblical vision. After such long and paralyzing conformity, Christians in community can begin to break free of their former attachments to the powers of the world as they come to understand their identity in Christ. The people of God is the central biblical metaphor in describing the believing community. Their communal life is to be directed by transcendent norms, and they are thus aliens who seek to "sing the Lord's song in a strange land." They are those who have been set free from the service of self, of principalities and powers, of idolatry and ideology, to form a new social reality that witnesses to the power of God unto salvation.

Creation of the Spirit

The Bible promises that, through the work of the Holy Spirit, God will raise up a faithful people to do what needs to be done. The origin of the church was at Pentecost when God poured out the Holy Spirit to fill the church and to empower its life and mission. The church is not expected to fulfill its mission in the world through its own strength or with mere human resources. It is meant to be the community of the Holy Spirit who was given to the church when the work of Christ had been accomplished. So the church is a house that the Lord builds, not one made with human hands.

As a creation of the Spirit, the church has a charismatic structure. That is, the church is a community organized according to neither hierarchy nor democracy but according to the gifts of the Spirit. These gifts are many and are given to the church richly and freely. Their purpose is to contribute to the upbuilding of the body and to enable the church to fulfill its mission in the world. Every member of the body has been endowed with spiritual gifts by virtue of his or her new life in Christ and is to use those gifts to build up the life and mission of the church which will be a practical demonstration of the reality and power of Jesus Christ in the world. Spiritual gifts are signs of the church and are the means of the church's transforming and healing power in the lives of its members and in the life of the nations. Through their exercise, the Christian community demonstrates to the world the possibilities of renewal and reconciliation. This community of the Spirit exists to minister in the name and power of Jesus to all the needs and brokenness of men and women. In the Book of Acts, the coming of the Spirit kindled not only spiritual renewal but social revolution.

Throughout Scripture, there is a vital relationship between the fullness of the Holy Spirit and the impulse and power to minister to the afflictions of the poor and the oppressed. Since the gifts of the Spirit are given to the church as new needs and situations arise, we can expect the renewal of the Spirit among us to empower us for new kinds of involvements in areas that have been largely ignored or given incomplete attention up to this point. The people of God will be given the gifts necessary for their mission in the world as they yield to their God in faithful obedience. Because the nature of our warfare with the principalities and powers of the world system is at root a spiritual battle (meaning that the sources of economic and political oppression derive from spiritual evil and demonic power, as in Eph. 6), the Christian community must learn not to fight them only with the same economic and political weapons they have at their disposal, but rather learn to employ spiritual resources and power and the gifts of the Spirit to resist their destructive purposes and consequences. The discovery of how to release and channel that kind of spiritual power in confrontation with institutional forces of injustice and violence is an undertaking to which we must address our prayers and our energy. We may find that new forms of gifts will be awakened among us as we seek to be the church in the midst of social and political realities that were not envisioned in the first century.

Not only may new manifestations of spiritual gifts be awakened among us but also new ways of expressing the classical charismatic gifts. It is important to remember that the gifts experienced within the primitive church did not come prepackaged with labels already attached. The manifestations happened; then Paul and others began naming them. Current styles of expressing certain of these gifts today may reflect more of a cultural habit than a biblical necessity. The gifts of the Spirit need not be restricted to the specific forms and styles of expression as they are now manifest in charismatic movements. For instance the gift of prophecy need not take the same form as it presently does, with a special prophetic vocabulary and rhetoric. As long as prophecy has to do with God's light on the present, edifying and consoling and reproving, the prophecy can take a number of different forms. I do not wish to minimize the importance and value of the charismatic gifts as they are currently experienced and expressed, but merely to help create an openness to new forms of gifts that may evolve among us.

The Holy Spirit is the source of community, and the Spirit's work is more related to the building of community than to the edification of the isolated individual.

Worship is more important to community and our involvements in the world than many of us ever recognized. In the New Testament, the "upbuilding" of community is almost always spoken of in connection with worship. A strong case can be made that the context where the Spirit most comes to visibility in building up the body of Christ is in the community gathered for worship. In a section of *Church Dogmatics* on "The Holy Spirit and the Upbuilding of the Christian Community," Karl Barth writes:

It is not only in worship that the community is edified . . . But it is here first that this continually takes place. If it does not edify itself here, it certainly will not do so in daily life, nor in the execution of its ministry in the world.

We have much to learn in recovering worship as the center and presupposition of the whole Christian life, the very atmosphere in which it is lived. Worship and the daily life of obedience of the Christian are not two separate spheres but two concentric circles, of which worship is the inner and gives to the outer its content and character.

Thus, at times, Scripture judges the value of worship, the inner circle, by looking at the shape of the outer circle, or the daily obedience it produces. Our worship should spread from the inner circle to the wider circle of our everyday lives as Christians, and our daily speech and acts and attitudes are ordained to be a wider and transformed worship.

The nature of our corporate worship will ultimately be a test of our other involvements in the world. The quality of our worship will reflect the quality of everything that we do, including whether we will serve and minister rightly in the world. If we are not experiencing the power of God in our worship with each other, we will not experience the power of God in our involvements in the world.

The work of the Holy Spirit is also central to ethical discernment. Throughout the Book of Acts, the Spirit is active especially in making decisions, and if the proportionate space given to various themes is indicative, the basic work of the Spirit (at least in Acts) is to guide in discernment, with prophecy, testimony, inward conviction, and empowerment for obedience and witness being subordinate aspects of that work. In *Christ and Time* (p. 228), Oscar Cullmann argues that the precise function of the Spirit is best summed up in Paul's word *dokimazo* (translated variously as "testing," "discerning," "proving," "determining"). "The working of the Holy Spirit shows itself chiefly in 'discerning,' that is, in the capacity of forming the correct Christian ethical judgment at each given moment. . . . This 'discerning' is the key to all New Testament ethics."

Though we understand the key to all New Testament ethics to be the kingdom of God and the teachings of Jesus, in the last analysis, there is not a conflict. Biblical scholarship recognizes that there exists an inner connection in Paul between the concepts "Spirit" and "kingdom of God" and that the role of the Spirit in Paul's teaching is similar to that of the kingdom in the Synoptics. Our concern about "kingdom ethics" and about recovering the ethic of Christ may be fruitfully enriched by exploring Paul's understanding of the Spirit.

Minister of Reconciliation

Alienation, conflict, enmity, brokenness, and fragmentation are the marks of our time. In contrast, reconciliation and new life are the message of the gospel. Restoration and setting right broken relationships is the work of reconciliation. Though the cross of Christ, God has made enemies into friends. We who had declared our enmity to God and to one another have now been reconciled to God and to each other through the work of Christ. The church of Jesus Christ is called to carry on the mission of Christ by serving as ministers of reconciliation.

To do so, we must be prepared to place ourselves where the alienation, tensions, and antagonisms are most severe. It is in the explosive and violent situations that the reconciling Christian presence is most needed. Reconciliation is not an easy task that can be achieved from a place of detachment, safety, and security. To act as ministers of reconciliation, the Christian community must establish itself on the front lines of chaos and human conflict. Such a presence can provide mediation, healing, redirection, change, and hope in an otherwise hopeless and destructive situation.

We must also be prepared to inject ourselves into the anguish and brokenness of people's lives. All around, people are suffering from personal fragmentation and emotional disorientation. Christian communities must provide environments of genuine and lasting healing which will attract those who are dying inside, those who long for love and acceptance, those who have no human warmth or intimacy in their lives. Many are longing to find people who would care about them enough to help them change their lives.

The basis of the reconciliation of persons is in the work of Christ in shattering former walls and barriers and creating a "new humanity." We must begin to comprehend the *social* character of justification and not only its personal meaning. Paul continually speaks of the "new creation" that has come in Christ and "breaks down the walls" between peoples. He tells the Jewish and Gentile Christians that they must live and worship together in unity or they are not being the church and are resisting the work of Christ. The apostle boldly proclaims that there is no longer Jew and Greek, slave and free, male and female, but that all have been made one in Christ Jesus (Gal. 3:28). Paul is here radically invalidating the pervasive divisions that have formerly kept people apart and led to oppression and conflict throughout history, namely, the facts of race, class, and sex. The Christian community is called to participate in Christ's work of abolishing these divisive and oppressive facts of history by first ending their influence in the church's life together. However, rather than overcome these barriers as the gospel commands, we have instead produced a church divided along the lines of race, ethnicity, and nationality; we have produced a church that closely conforms to the class and caste structures which surround it; and we have so organized the life of the church as to deny full expression and personhood to half of its membership—those who are women. How can we ever serve as ministers of reconciliation if we merely reflect and reproduce the divisions and cleavages of the world system?

Those who have been excluded, exploited, and manipulated by the established institutions of a social order will eventually rise up in revolt in the name of new idolatries to replace the old ones which have failed. This is a historical inevitability. The ongoing problem of any established order is to keep its victims somehow content, resigned, and passive while continuing to pursue the course of its own power, consumption, and manipulation. Conflict normally results when the established groups continue their self-appropriation, never having enough of their chosen idolatries, while oppressed groups continue to demand new conditions and relationships as necessary for their own survival, aspirations, and fulfillment. Injustice and oppression will, in the course of time, always breed dissent and revolt. Such is the nature of the human spirit.

Justice and reconciliation become severely diminished when the groups and institutions of the established order refuse to allow meaningful change to take place when the insurgents opt for violence and the tactics of destruction. The Scriptures describe this situation as "the hardening of the heart." Channels for necessary mediation and fundamental social change have been blocked and closed. Such a situation now exists in many parts of the world and inevitably results in violent revolutionary conflict. When revolution breaks out in a closed situation of great alienation and injustice, the church may understand it as the wrath of God upon the insensitivity and corruption of a social order in which the rich and powerful have refused to allow necessary changes to come about peacefully.

The only place for the Christian community, in such a situation, is in the midst of the conflict. Merely to condemn and criticize revolution from a position of comfort, safety, and privilege, as a beneficiary of the injustice and violence of the established order, is to engage in hypocrisy. When Christians cease to feel any identification with the hopes, goals, and aspirations of revolutionary movements, it may be because they have also ceased to understand the revolutionary character of their own faith and the compassion of Christ for the world. Christians too should see reality of the world's appalling conditions and oppressive circumstances and discern the need for change of a revolutionary kind. Jesus associated closely with many from the Zealot movement whose revolutionary political option constituted his greatest source of temptation. His denunciation of the religious and the political establishment and his radical identification with the poor often led the authorities to mistake him for a Zealot. Why is it that most churches today would most identify, not with the insurgent movements of the poor and the oppressed, but rather with the values and institutions of the established order—an option which was never any temptation for Jesus? Perhaps the reason that modern Christians are seldom mistaken for contemporary Zealots, as Jesus was, is that we have ceased to understand or participate in the compassion of Christ for the world and especially for the poor and exploited masses.

However, the Christian community must avoid the false assumption, as did Jesus, that the salvation and liberation of the world come through violence and force, that the means of the kingdom are compatible with the means of death. Jesus' ultimate rejection of the Zealot option teaches that those using the force of arms will not usher in the kingdom, that the way of Christ is the way of servanthood, or reconciliation, of a cross—not a sword. The central and debilitating failure of revolution to bring genuine liberation lies in its reliance upon the same moral authority and instrumental means of the established order and systems it seeks to overthrow—namely, death.

This moral dependence upon death that is inherent in every violent revolution is a deeper issue than simply the revolution's failure to live up to its initial promises, its corruption and distortions of original goals, its abandonment of revolutionary aims for the "realistic" requirements of a new regime. Rather, the dependence upon death is the source of those many infirmities. The moral authority and rule of death is present in the inception of revolution and is at the root of every revolution's ultimate failure to be truly revolutionary. The American and Soviet revolutions are prime examples. Violence is a consequence of the fall; in fact, it is the instrumental means of the fallen creation. Violence is the reign and instrumentality of death, in all its forms. Violence is hardly restricted to the outbreak of gunfire but is present in all the broken relationships, all the injustice of institutions, all the confusion and chaos, all the oppressive conditions, all the circumstances of human suffering, all the falsehood and babel of the world system. Therefore, the counterviolence of revolution can never undo the violence of the system but can only continue and perpetuate the rule of death in the world, perhaps in a different form. Jacques Ellul has said that every act of violence, no matter how small and no matter for what purpose, has the moral effect of increasing the prevalence and power of violence in the world. There are, therefore, no wars to end wars, no wars which humanize and liberate, no just wars, no just revolutions, no violence of glory and salvation. As A. J. Muste once said, "There is no road to peace, peace is the road."

Though the cycle of violence and counterviolence may be used against itself by God in judgment, correction, and the opening up of closed social situations, revolution itself, because of its reliance upon violence and death, will never remove the sources of alienation or bring reconciliation.

The patterns of alienation and injustice will again reassert themselves, often very soon, sometimes as violently and as destructively as before or maybe more so. The problem with revolution is not that it is too radical but that it is not radical enough, not that it changes things too much but that it doesn't change things enough. It can revise or reverse the structures of idolatry and alienation but never eradicate them. It may change the patterns of production and distribution but leave untouched the roots of the human condition, the roots of those patterns.

The mission of reconciliation in the midst of revolution must be to affirm the ultimate goals and aspirations of revolution but, at the same time, to confront, expose, and puncture the false myths and idolatries of the revolution itself. The assumption that all the alienation and injustice of the society are due to the powerful and their institutions whose rule is the only obstacle to righteousness, peace, and justice must be countered with a more profound understanding of human sin and idolatry in order to prepare people for the inevitable disillusionment that will come later. Christians must defend the humanity of the "counterrevolutionaries," maintaining themselves as a community of love and reconciliation that refuses to break fellowship with people on the basis of their relationship to the revolution. It is a superficial understanding that attempts to suppress tyranny by crushing the oppressor class. Though Christians may see God at work in revolution, they will be skeptical of revolutionary promises which have historically produced far less than they have promised. As Christians cannot sanctify the values and structures of the status quo, neither can they baptize every expression of revolutionary violence to soothe their feelings of guilt for past failures. Again, our problem today is a too easy conformity to one secular option or another rather than seeking alternatives that may be more biblically rooted. The church's task is not to rush in to join the revolution and uncritically accept the new idolatries it proclaims. To do so is to continue to make the church subservient to the secular order, to confuse its identity with nations, movements, and ideologies, to continue to believe that God "is on our side" (or perhaps, now, that he has switched sides), to repeat the mistakes of the Constantinian synthesis of church and society in merely a different form, to forget its primary task of witness to the radical presence of the kingdom of God, to forget that its Lord demonstrated and commissioned a different strategy to challenge and conquer the forces of alienation, injustice, violence, and death.

Though Christ did not join himself to the Zealots, he left no question as to whether he was on the side of the poor and oppressed or whether he was on the side of the power structures of his time. The political and religious authorities judged him to be criminal and executed him as a subversive. The option of violence against the poor (which is what American power at home and abroad is all about) or the option of collaboration with the established authorities were never options that tempted Christ. On the other hand, the Zealot option of revolutionary violence was clearly a constant temptation and tension throughout his ministry. As previously noted, the fact that the reverse is true in most quarters of the church today and that few contemporary Christians are mistaken for Zealots is an issue that bears directly on how we regard the authority of Christ.

While Jesus was wrongly accused of assuming the role of the Messianic leader of an armed revolt, he was rightly accused of taking the side of the poor against the established political and religious authorities. Our nonviolence must be equally credible and equally revolutionary if it is to be after the pattern and spirit of Christ. If our nonviolence is being ideologically used against the poor, if our stance is passive and peacefully coexists with the violence of the oppressive order against the poor, or if we benefit and profit from the suffering of others while we preach nonviolence, then the violence of the poor condemns us.

If we would follow Christ and give our nonviolence integrity, we must make very sure that our choices and actions will set us on the side of the poor and be so clearly made that we will be likely to be convicted of subversion of the established order. The actions of Christ are clearly rooted in his self-understanding as suffering servant. He points his community to the same path, to renounce the struggle for wealth and power, and to give themselves over to the poor and the oppressed. Jesus sets aside the force of arms and the road to political power for the way of the cross and the victory of the resurrection as a sign of God's new age of liberation and reconciliation. In Christ there is a necessary relationship between nonviolence and suffering. His community of reconciliation must therefore be a community of suffering. The first community the church must have with the poor is a community of suffering.

A fundamental attitude characterizes both the rulers of the established order and the leaders of a revolution, that is, the subordination of persons to causes. This the Christian community must refuse to do. The path of revolutionary violence is not wrong simply because it employs the wrong means to bring in a new order, but that the order it produces is not new. The means are always integrally bound up with the ends. An order brought into being by violence and death cannot be an alternative to the established order sustained by the same weapons. Revolutionary violence in response to the oppression and violence of the established order is another form of assimilating the values of the system and the militant power of death over life in the world. Recourse to the means of violence preserves the unbroken cycle of idolatry because its perpetrators seek salvation and reconciliation apart from the means God has chosen to transform and remake the world, the style of servanthood, love, sacrifice, and the way of the cross. While the world rushes to take up sides and define "the other" as the enemy, Jesus readily associated with all manner of men and women, Zealot and publican, sinners and priests, Jew and Roman, poor and rich. In doing so, he made enemies into friends, and by being obedient unto death he accomplished the great work of salvation, transforming those who had made themselves "enemies" of God into the children of God, reconciled and made new. All this he accomplished, not by might and power, but as he "emptied himself, taking the form of a servant, . . . and became obedient unto death, even the death of the cross." Biblical politics must take the style and action of Jesus as the key to understanding the Christian relationship to society, to power, to revolution, and to social change. William Stringfellow comments lucidly on that style:

Meanwhile, there is the problem symbolized in the First Century by the zealots. The relationship between the Christians and the zealots, is poignant because the Christians, faced with the reality of a decadent and repressive State, discern, as lucidly as the zealots, the pathetic need for change of revolutionary magnitude and scope. Yet the Christian pauses over the tactics of the zealots. Revolutionary violence which overthrows the violence of the State can itself only become a regime of violence. Tactics cannot be severed from ethics, and imitation of the enemy is the most common way in which ideology has been confounded, idealism corrupted, and revolutions rendered futile. The Christian perseveres in nonviolent actions of protest and resistance—

shunning whatever increases the work of death—in the hope of thereby calling into being new forms of life in society. And if, sometimes, as in the First Century, that means the Christian becomes as much a victim of the hostility and assault of the zealots as of the State, then so be it (*Suspect Tenderness*, pp. 83–84).

And again,

The direct political implication of this risen character of the Christian is that, as contrasted with other revolutionaries, of which Barabbas is the example and symbol, the Christian is an incessant revolutionary. He is always, everywhere, in revolt—not for himself but for humanity. There is something inherently, invariably, persistently, perpetually, inexhaustibly, inevitably revolutionary in the suffering of reconciliation— in the experience of one's own personhood as humanity in society— which constitutes the Christian life in this world. The Christian as revolutionary is constantly welcoming the gift of human life, for himself and for all men, by exposing, opposing, and overturning all that betrays, entraps, or attempts to kill human life. The difference between Christ and Barabbas as revolutionaries is the difference between life and death as both the imminent reality and the ultimate value of revolution (*Suspect Tenderness*, pp. 63–64).

To be an advocate of human life rather than of causes and ideologies, to witness to the kingdom, will gain one few friends. It will mean to be looked upon by the established order as a subversive, and sometimes by the revolution as an obstructionist and maybe even a counterrevolutionary. But not to persist in the ministry of reconciliation is to allow the hope of new life to be extinguished by the cycle of idolatry and the power of death which seeks to surround and swallow it up.

The Power of Servanthood

Have this mind among yourselves, which you have in Christ Jesus, who though he was in the form of God, did not count equality with God a thing to be grasped, but emptied himself, taking the form of a servant, being born in the likeness of men. And being found in human form he humbled himself and became obedient unto death, even the death on a cross. Therefore

God has highly exalted him and bestowed on him the name which is above every name, that at the name of Jesus every knee should bow, in heaven and on earth and under the earth, and every tongue confess that Jesus Christ is Lord, to the Glory of God the Father (Phil. 2:5–11, RSV).

You know that in the world, rulers lord it over their subjects, and their great men make them feel the weight of authority; but it shall not be so with you. Among you, whoever wants to be great must become your servant, and whoever wants to be first must be the willing slave of all—like the Son of Man; he did not come to be served, but to serve, and to give his life as a ransom for many (Matt. 20:25–28, NEB).

The great scandal of the New Testament is the cross. The world's enduring trust in and eternal striving for political and military power is scandalized by the servanthood of God. God enters human history, not as one who exercises political authority and force of arms, but in the form of a servant. While most historiography focuses on rulers, generals, dynasties, empires, battles, elections, the wealthy, and the powerful, the biblical witness claims that the central meaning of history is revealed in the person who became one with the poor and vulnerable, who lived in the world as a suffering servant, who rejected the temptations of political and military power, who exercised his kingship by washing his disciples feet and giving his life so that others might live.

This biblical theme is ably stated in Jürgen Moltmann's book, *The Crucified God*:

Now the death of Christ was the death of a political offender. According to the scale of social values of the time, crucifixion was dishonour and shame. If this crucified man has been raised from the dead and exalted to be the Christ of God, then what public opinion holds to be lowliest, what the state has determined to be disgraceful is changed into what is supreme. In that case, the glory of God does not shine on the crowns of the mighty, but on the face of the crucified Christ. The authority of God is then no longer represented directly by those in high positions, the powerful and the rich, but by the outcast Son of

Man, who died between two wretches. The rule and the kingdom of God are no longer reflected in political rule and world kingdoms, but in the service of Christ, who humiliated himself to the point of death on the cross. The consequences for Christian theology is that it must adopt a critical attitude towards political religions in society and in the churches. The political theology of the cross must liberate the state from the poltical service of idols and must liberate men from political alienation and loss of rights. It must seek to demythologize state and society. It must prepare for the revolution of all values which is involved in the exaltation of the crucified Christ, in the demoltion of relationships of political domination (p. 327).

No longer can we avoid what the implications of the servanthood of God in Jesus Christ hold for the political witness of the church. The grasping of the church for political and even military power in an attempt to gain control and influence in its society is a direct contradiction to the way of Christ. When we strive for power on the world's terms, we merely demonstrate our degree of conformity with the systems and ideologies of the world and show our acceptance of their definitions of what is important and what constitutes greatness. The New Testament sees greatness not as the exercise of political authority and military might, but as the willingness to serve others even at great personal cost and sacrifice. Jesus' kingship is exercised as servanthood. He unites the concepts of leader and servant. Jesus is the servant king, and if we are his people, we must be a servant people. The question here is nothing less than how we regard the authority of Jesus Christ.

The notion of "Christian responsibility" has suffered much distortion and abuse in recent times. In seeking to be responsible to the world, many have come to accept the world's own assumptions and norms of what responsibility is. The accepted canons of political realism and economic necessity that prevail in the world's ideological systems have increasingly dominated the discussions of what would constitute responsible Christian action in the world. That the Christian community must live and act responsibly in the world is beyond question, as is the fact that Christians have a special and a decisive responsibility to the ongoing life of the world. The critical question is: Who or what determines the shape of responsible Christian action in the world? Do our norms for action derive from what the world considers to be helpful, necessary, realistic, relevant, and responsible, or do the norms of Christian responsibility derive from the biblical witness and, most crucially, from the manner of the life and death of Jesus Christ in the world? The shape of his responsibility was in adopting the posture of a servant and going to a cross.

For those who would seriously confess Jesus as Lord, the posture of a servant and the way of the cross is politically axiomatic. If responsibility demands that we exercise power and authority on the world's terms, then Christ must be accused of failing to live up to his Christian responsibilities. It would be hard to demonstrate from the New Testament that Jesus was a "Christian realist." When our definition of Christian responsibility requires that we opt for the exercise of the same political and military power that Jesus rejected, we are beginning to question the authority of the incarnation and the efficacy of the very means God has chosen for the salvation and reconciliation of the world. To set aside the manner of Jesus' life and death because of other factors or considerations is to establish "other lights" of revelation that compete with Christ for our obedience.

The gospel of Jesus Christ calls us to live responsibly before God in the world. Clearly, the way we are to assume responsibility in the world is by following Jesus. However, the style of the crucified suffering servant does not lend itself well to the usual kind of actions and approaches that our normal perception of the human condition and the requirements of political reality would deem as responsible. This dilemma of responsibility is a major problem. The New Testament suggests again and again that obedience rather than effectiveness and calculated success is the criterion of faith. This "different logic" of the gospel runs counter to what comes most naturally to us and is a scandal to all ideological and political necessities. Our conflict is this: it seems to us impossible to be both what the world's political realities set forth as "responsible" and to take up the style of the crucified servant which is clearly the manner of the life and death of Jesus Christ as revealed in the New Testament.

Theology has gone through endless contortion and distortion in its attempts to resolve this dilemma. The most troublesome biblical passages have been ignored, neglected, or given evasive exegesis. Jesus' radical ethic has been locked up in the past as a confused "interim" ethic or projected into the future as merely an apocalyptic ethic, both in an attempt to keep the kingdom ethic out of the present. Jesus has been recreated into a political messiah, ignoring his rejection of both the Saducees' attempts to bring change through the political realism of compromise and collaboration with the system and the Zealot attempts at a revolutionary overthrow. He has been reduced to the "personal Savior" of private justification, thus denying the kingdom message at the heart of the New Testament and stripping away the discipleship imperative. Others talk of a "special vocation" through a subbiblical assumption of a separation of clergy and laity. Still others refer to the "impossible possibility" of Christ, rendering our Lord irrelevant to political activity. This approach restricts Christ to the personal, individual level while deriving its social action from the world's accepted norms and canons of political and economic "responsibility." It is a serious attack upon the lordship of Christ over all of human life and affairs which, in the New Testament, is not only a personal but a structural and political fact of reality.

The trouble with all these solutions is that they avoid the offense of Jesus' life and death or they deny the incarnation by making Jesus into a special kind of person who did not have to bear the burdens of human life in society, those burdens of social and political responsibility for which the rest of us are held accountable. When the concrete meaning of Christ in history is set aside for reasons of responsibility on the world's terms, the various strategies of realpolitik come to replace the style of servanthood in the life of the church.

Most of these discussions fail to recognize that the posture of servanthood is not a posture of nonpower. Rather, the servant style of life and action is an *alternative mode of power*. It rests

upon the power of truth, the power of dissent, the power of with-
holding confidence, the power of unmasking idolatry, the power of
an alternative vision, the power of sacrifice and perseverance, the
power of healing and reconciliation, the power of creativity in
offering new signs, building new models, pioneering new ideas, the
power of moral independence enabling conscientious objection or
conscientious participation in secular structures for a prophetic
witness, the power to suffer evil and violence rather than inflicting
it, the power of serving human life with one's only compensation
being the joy that comes from obedience, the power of resistance
and celebration. The posing and the living of alternatives beyond
the range of "acceptable options" is precisely what the political
process most needs. Fundamental change comes through a leaven-
ing process originating from groups at the peripheries or at the
bottom of society, groups who live and act out of different commitments and values than the rest of society. Their presence is a
decisive force that must be dealt with by those who exercise political power. They are usually outside the spectrum of "responsible
opinion" and "viable options," but they are the ones whose presence and action becomes the greatest catalyst for social change. It
is the conformity to "acceptable options" that extinguishes the
possibility and promise of fundamental change.

The occasion for Jesus' discourse on the human temptation of
power (Matt. 20 and Mark 10) comes when some of his disciples
ask him for promises of prestige and power in the kingdom. Here
the disciples were asking for the very same thing they despised in
those who ruled over them. This shows the great attraction and
temptation that power holds for us. We repeat the mistake of the
disciples when we seek greater power and control in the world so
that, of course, we can use the power for good. Jesus teaches in
the passages that those in power always claim to be benefactors,
to be using their power for good which becomes their justification
for using any and all means to protect and expand their power.
Jesus simply sets that claim aside and teaches his followers to
renounce the power game altogether and seek greatness in serving
and seeking first the kingdom. Jesus is the king who puts himself

at the disposal of others, whose cross is the means of his rule, whose resurrection is the victory of his reign. The sign of his sovereignty is the serving and suffering which we must participate in if we would share in his reign.

The alternative to participate in Christ's sovereignty by way of serving is to exercise our own sovereignty. It is to believe along with Caiaphas that the end justifies the means and that a desirable social goal can be achieved through unethical means. The very political power that we strive so desperately to possess is the very power that was used to crucify Jesus Christ. The calculating ethics of compromising means for the sake of anticipated ends is the rationale that was used to justify the murder of our Lord. "It is expedient for us that one man should die for the people and that the whole nation should perish not."

The New Testament ethic is based upon obedience and faithfulness, not upon expedience and calculation. We have neither the insight nor the moral right to choose to compromise with evil so that good might result. To do so is to exercise our own sovereignty rather than trusting in God's and is to confuse our responsibility for obedience with the utilitarian principle of "making history come out right." That responsibility is God's alone. Our part in God's action in history is to be a servant people who live in radical obedience to Jesus Christ in whom is revealed God's will for human life and society. Faith is the willingness to pursue the seemingly ineffectual path of obedience and trusting God for the results. The cross is our example and pattern, the seeming defeat that was turned into the greatest victory in history through the power of God in the resurrection of Jesus Christ. Faith lives by the means of a cross and through the power of a resurrection. Yoder comments on the servant people:

What the world most needs is not a new Caesar but a new style. A style is created, updated, projected, not by a nation or a government, but by a people. This is what moral minorities can do.—what they have done time and again.

Liberation is not a new King; we've tried that. Liberation is the presence of a new option, and only a non-conformed, covenanted people of God can offer that. Liberation is the pressure of the presence of a new alternative so valid, so coherent, that it can live without the props of power and against the stream of statesmanship. To be that option is to be free indeed. (*Cross Currents*, Fall 1973).

Prophetic Minority

The church's calling is not to become a power of the world exercising influence in the same way and by the same methods as the powers and institutions of the world system. Rather, the church must remember the pitfalls of its own history, stand firmly on the ground of revelation, and maintain the independence and free perspective required to be obedient to its prophetic role and calling. If the church is too dependent upon the values, securities, institutions, and methods of its social order, it will be unable to raise the prophetic witness so desperately needed by that social order. Rather than softening the demands of the gospel to gain majority acceptance and recognition, the church must accept its biblical calling as a minority body which serves the world not by conforming to it but by calling people to new possibilities of human life.

When the church begins to forsake its basis in God's revelation, it robs itself of its basis for speaking prophetically. In an ill-advised attempt to make Christian faith more acceptable, the churches may depreciate the centrality of the revelation of the Word of God which only results in the church's forfeiting the right and the insight to make meaningful ethical judgments. Therefore, a recovery of the church's prophetic mission necessarily entails a recovery of its revelational basis.

On the other hand, when the church affirms the need of a revelatory basis for ethical judgments but is blinded to the relevance of that revelation in its life and in its society, it virtually denies the existence of revelation. To ignore or deny the application and meaning of revelation to concrete social and political circumstances is at least as harmful as denying the possibility of revelation altogether. Revelation must become the basis for ethical judgment and action rather than a substitution for it.

At the heart of the message of Jesus was the proclamation of the kingdom of God. The kingdom is the reign of Christ where righteousness, peace, and justice are the predominant characteristics. We are called to seek it above all else, to pray for its coming, to expect to find it already present among us, to live in its promise, to look forward to the day when the kingdoms of this world will become the kingdoms of our Lord.

Instead, the churches have secularized the kingdom by identifying it with ideologies, programs, movements, institutions, and governments; they have individualized it by restricting it to inner recesses of the heart; they have spiritualized it by removing it entirely to heaven; or they have futurized it by speaking of it only in connection with apocalyptic events at the end of time.

All this ignores the biblical understanding of the kingdom which sees its reality as both present and future. Though the kingdom will only come with full power and authority with God's final consummation, the biblical promise is that we can begin to live in the reality of the kingdom now. Though the kingdom is future, it can break into history with explosive force and power. Because the ultimate triumph of the kingdom is sure, we are freed not to live according to the world's standards but to participate boldly in its coming. The church is called to be the first fruits of the kingdom, a body of people who can begin to taste now what God wills for human life and society. The church is the nucleus of those who have accepted and welcomed the message of the kingdom and whose task it is to bear witness to it. The church heralds the coming of the kingdom and is an anticipatory sign of it. The church is a community that lives in light of the coming kingdom and, as such, will be a radical nonconformist community in the present world system, refusing to live by the norms and assumptions that control the behavior of others. The life of the new community, then, is directed by the priorities of Christ and his kingdom and is to be a sign of the new creation that is coming and is already in the making.

The Christian message is about the future of humankind that has already come in Jesus Christ. A new order has invaded history and will eventually come to fulfillment. In other words, a revolu-

tion of human life and society has already begun, and we participate in it by beginning to live in its promise. By the acceptance of
the meaning of that revolution in our lives, we are no longer to be
clinging to the past, resigned to the present, or fearful of the
future. Our expectation and confidence in the future comes from
the reality of our own transformation into "a new humanity' and
is a radicalism that is not easily crushed by opposition. We have
been freed to serve and to create new alternatives because we now
participate in the nature and power of the new order. We are those
who live in the present reality and future promise of a revolution
that is already undermining the structure of the present world
system.

All this gives the Christian community a prophetic mission in
the life of the world.

The new community must witness to the fact that Christ has
triumphed over the principalities and powers of the world system
(Col. 2:15). The rebellious powers have been disarmed by Christ
and their final defeat is sure. The structures of class, race, sex,
ideology, government, money, and power need not determine us
any longer. The victory of Christ liberates people from their slavery. Their ultimate authority has been broken. The Christian
community is called to show the reality of the victory of Christ
over the powers of the world. It is to visibly demonstrate that the
dominion of these powers is no longer absolute and unchallenged.
It is to make hope and change visible to those who still live under
the oppression of the powers. The church's responsibility is to
defy and resist the powers when they overstep their modest limited
purposes, when they make absolute claim for themselves, when
they seek control over men and women, when they command
action contrary to the kingdom which alone has ultimate authority
for the Christian community. The fundamental style of participat-
ing in the kingdom is the way of the cross, after the pattern of
Christ's victory over the principalities and powers.

To be an active agent of the kingdom is our highest calling. The
kingdom generates new forces of righteousness, justice, and peace
through the means of servanthood and self-giving love. We must

be willing to give our lives, all of our lives, in allegiance to the kingdom regardless of the cost. When we do that, we begin to have a part in breaking the cycle of death and dehumanization that now dominates the world system; we begin to reject our assigned roles in the present scheme of things. We begin to test all things by a biblical judgment, and the church is slowly led from conformity and convulsion to community and change. In all this, we will begin to regain possession of ourselves from the world so that we can offer ourselves to the service of Christ and his kingdom.

The kingdom is within and among us; it is our standard, our calling, our hope, and our salvation. It is deeper, stronger, more profound and lasting than all our programs, strategies, projects, and causes. When we forget our primary call to be a sign of the kingdom, our causes and our very selves become captive and part of the old order, however noble our intentions. The kingdom breaks into history, and the old order quickly seeks to surround the signs of the new and to swallow them up with conformity and destruction.

Therefore, we must be people of prayer and discernment, those with the ability to search beneath the surface of concrete situations for signs of hope and change. In doing so, we must learn to discern and articulate movements of the Spirit and bring clarification to confusion. We must have the courage to question all that is on the basis of what we have seen beyond the present confusion and injustice. We must live in the world without conforming to it, in the midst of people without conforming to them. The Christian community must be a place where the vicious cycle of immediate needs, concerns, and problems is broken through a vision that can perceive the truth in concrete situations, establish priorities, and apprehend future directions.

Thus, our prophetic mission must be spiritually discerning and deeply sensitive to the forces of history and the workings of the Spirit. We need to do more than simply respond to events and crises after they have reached the front pages of the daily newspaper. For then it is often too late to avert catastrophe and suffering. Rather, we should warn about the dangerous consequences of present historical patterns and choices. We must not let the world entirely determine our agenda. We must set our own agenda in human affairs that derives from our asking what the Word of God says concerning the conditions and circumstances of our own history and of our own lives. Movements that are merely "political" are born and die as things change. Movements that are merely "spiritual" in an inward way fail to come to grips with political realities. Only that which has a deep spiritual base and active political sensitivities can be prophetic in the biblical sense.

The task of the Christian revolution is not only to change and reform the economic and political facts and form of the world, but to seek fundamental change in the very framework and structure of a world system that needs to be continually examined and tested by the judgment of the Word of God. Such an undertaking will often result in profound political and economic changes but is essentially a more pervasive and perpetual mission than the effecting of a series of social changes. All of these social changes will be temporary and limited in scope and, while they are important, are never to be thought to satisfy the more absolute demands of the kingdom. The Christian community can never be satisfied with social achievements and progress and must continue to assert the claim of God upon the world and the ultimate will of God that righteousness, peace, and justice prevail in human affairs. In a world that always tends toward injustice and disorder, the Christian community will be an unceasing agent of change, a continual center of questioning, dissent, and opposition to the idolatries of the established order, a perpetual advocate of human life in the midst of a world still dominated by death. In so doing, the Christian community becomes an inexhaustible revolutionary force in the life of the world, never content to conform to history, prepared only to give its ultimate allegiance to the kingdom of God which is coming and is made a present reality by the faithfulness and obedience of the people of God.

Jacques Ellul cogently describes "the revolutionary situation" of the Christian community.

In reality all solutions, all economic, political, and other achievements are temporary. At no moment can the Christian believe either in their perfection or in their permanence. They are always vitiated by the sin which infects them, by the setting in which they take place. Thus the Christian is constantly obliged to reiterate the claims of God, to re-establish this God-will 'order,' in presence of an order which constantly tends towards disorder. In consequence of the claims which God is always making on the world the Christian finds himself, by that very fact, involved in a state of permanent revolution. Even when the institutions, the laws, the reforms which he had advocated have been achieved, even if society be re-organized according to his suggestions, he still has to be in opposition, he still must exact more, for the claim of God is as infinite as His forgiveness. Thus the Christian is called to question unceasingly all that man calls progress, discovery, fact, established results, reality, etc. He can never be satisfied with all this human labour, and in consequence he is always claiming that it should be transcended, or replaced by something else.

In his judgment he is guided by the Holy Spirit—he is making an essentially revolutionary act. If the Christian is not being revolutionary, then in some way or another he has been unfaithful to his calling in the world (*Presence of the Kingdom*, pp. 48, 49).

Ellul continues,

This then is the revolutionary situation: to be revolutionary is to judge the world by its present state, by actual facts, in the name of a truth which does not yet exist (but which is coming)—and it is to do so, because we believe this truth to be more genuine and more real than the reality which surrounds us. Consequently it means bringing the future into the present as an explosive force. It means believing that future events are more important and truer than present events; it means understanding the present in the light of the future, dominating it by the future in the same way as the historian dominates the past (*Presence of the Kingdom*, pp. 50, 51).

The Christian is motivated by hope for the kingdom and is to look for the manifestation of that future in the present. Christians are to live "as in the day" (Rom. 13:13). What the apostle means is that Christians are to live here and now with the knowledge that the coming kingdom is already present among us. We are to embody in the present the priorities of that coming kingdom. In doing so, the Christian is the herald and harbinger of the revolution that will ultimately transform the whole of human life when the kingdoms of this world will become the kingdoms of Christ (Rev. 11:15). Though we cannot bring in the kingdom by our actions, we witness to it by beginning to give its values concrete expression. This has important implications. It means that we must not conform to the past nor to the status quo of the present order. We are not limited to the definitions and options and strategies which are available in the world. We are freed to live in light of the future which has been revealed in Jesus Christ. He is the sign of what is coming, and we must be also by living lives which witness to what the kingdom will bring forth.

The central biblical tension between "this age" and "the age to come" is the political key, the decisive factor of radical social change in history. Revolution is founded upon the premise that something is basically wrong with the world and springs from a vision of change and hope that has been seen beyond the present circumstances and conditions of history. Confident faith in the power of a future reality is hardly a social opiate that encourages passive acceptance of the status quo, but rather is the very engine and dynamo of revolutionary expectation and action.

In a world that does not know God, the church lives in radical antagonism to the existing order of things. The Bible sees the powers of the world in rebellion against God and in domination over human life. The Bible names the prince of the world as the Devil. The church of Jesus Christ is at war with the systems of the world, not détente, ceasefire, or peaceful coexistence, but at war. The church exists to continually confront the world with a new reality—the kingdom of God—that has invaded the world and taken root in the life of the church as God's new community.

Because of its own revolt against the existing order, the obedient church has a deep sympathy for all the revolters of the world. Though rejecting their new myths and idolatries, refusing their ideological visions based upon false human hopes, and regarding their means of violence and death as signs of their conformity to the world, the faithful church keenly feels the oppression and aspirations of those who revolt against the established order of things. The church has the unique and crucial role in history of viewing the systems and institutions of the world through the eyes of their *victims*. Since all the systems of the world have their victims, which is quickly discovered when a revolutionary movement becomes the new regime, identification with the victims is a perpetual task. The church must serve, stand with, plead the cause, and defend the life and value of all those who have been victimized for ideological, economic, or political reasons.

In order that the church be faithful to its revolutionary mission, it is absolutely necessary that it accept its minority status in a hostile world. It is "official," "established," "majority" Christianity that represents the "fall" of the church, that betrays the identity of the people of God, that corrupts and cheapens the kingdom by making it into a secular reality. The call for the restitution and restoration of the true and authentic church has been the battle cry whenever the church makes its peace with the world, whenever it ceases to exist for the changing of the world, but rather for the legitimating of it in its present circumstances, which is the meaning of "Christendom."

The church's biblical identity is not the clerical vassal of the social order but the vanguard and vehicle of the coming kingdom. The obedient church is on the front lines of God's action in history bringing about the radical transformation of human life and history. The church is the sign and bearer of the new order. The Christian community fulfills its mission, not by conforming to the world's definitions of "responsibility" and "realism," but by bringing the presence and power of the kingdom right into the midst of current social and political realities with explosive consequences. The moving power of history has never been conformity to present circumstances and political "realities." The primary engine of social change is disciplined and sacrificing minorities whose alternative vision, style of life, and radical action demand a response that moves history. The church is that prophetic minority when it lives faithfully to its calling in the world. The social and political meaning of the kingdom makes the church into this dynamic minority.

Our actions must announce the coming kingdom. Our style of life must testify to the coming kingdom. The church must live in the world in such a way that the kingdom "breaks in" bringing radical change and transformation in history. Seeking first the kingdom is the crux of discipleship and is an eternal revolutionary posture, never satisfied with less than all that God wills for human life and society, always aspiring to the most radical change in the lives of men and women and in the life of the world. The church continues to articulate a critical vision of the social and political realities of the present world. The church refuses to make any political reality or particular social order an absolute by identifying it with the kingdom of God. The Christian community is engaged in the demythologizing and debunking of the ideological idolatry that substitutes a secular vision for the kingdom of God (in Facism, Marxism, Capitalism, Liberal Democracy, various nationalisms, and so on). The critical function, however, is not limited to dissent and the proclaiming of God's judgment on false human hopes. It is also the action of creating structures and relationships which are more serving of human life, justice, and freedom, even while not assigning an absolute value to such efforts. The church's critical function, in both negative judgment and in building alternatives, is prophetic as a demonstration in history of God's love and purposes for human life in the world. To surrender the critical function is to capitulate to the world and its false and destructive illusions about its ability to save itself apart from God's action in history.

Jesus rejected the major options of his day: identification with the religious and political establishment (the Sadducees), the path of proper religious observance (the Pharisees), the quietistic possibility of withdrawing from conflict and tension to a place of comfort and noninvolvement (the Essenes), and the movement toward violent revolution (the Zealots). Instead, he chose another option. He preached the judgment of God upon the present order and heralded the coming of a new order, then called into being a community of faith that would witness to the hope and power of that new order and already began to make its presence felt in the world. This was continuous with the purposes of God throughout history: to call out a faithful people, set apart from the world but radically involved in it as witnesses to and agents of God's salvation in history. This is what John Howard Yoder calls "the original revolution; the creation of a distinct community with its own set of deviant values and its coherent way of incarnating them." This community would be the one "that has not made itself one with the nations," (Num. 23:9) but would demonstrate by its own life and action a whole new order in human affairs called the kingdom of God. It would be a voluntary society made up of those who have given their lives over to Christ and his kingdom. It would be a mix of humankind, breaking down the barriers of class, race, and sex. It would be centered around a new way of life and a new way of responding by forgiving its enemies, sharing its money freely, being willing to suffer violence rather than inflicting it, resisting the temptation of power by adopting the posture of a servant, evoking leadership through the gifts of the body, responding to evil by overcoming it with good, confronting the state by its moral independence and prophetic witness, and challenging the old society by building a new one.

This would be the way that God would remake the world and bring reconciliation to men and women. This new peoplehood would be "salt" and "light" in a world bound to sin and death. The very existence of such a community is a profound threat to the established order and an ever-present catalyst for fundamental social change if it remains faithful to its calling. To proclaim and to live in the light of the future that has already come in Christ undermines the present structure of a world system that cannot tolerate nonconformity. The presence of a people who are not playing by the accepted rules of the game creates serious disruption and calls the whole meaning of the game into question. The Christian community is the ultimate parallel institution, a group within a society constantly confronting all other groups with models of life and hope while demonstrating the possibility of human community.

Epilogue: Sojourners in the Land

The intensity of the problems we face today render traditional approaches and solutions inadequate and counterproductive. The brutal realities of global poverty, new alignments of repressive power, economic systems that ravage the environment and crush the poor, political corruption, the escalation of violence in all its forms, the ugly spirit of racism and sexism, the uniformity of technology accompanied by the loss of human freedom and dignity, and the social disintegration, boredom, and meaninglessness of affluent mass societies all point to the moral bankruptcy of traditional solutions and established leadership. The continual promises of those in power and of those who aspire to power suggesting that solutions are just around the corner have proved illusory and deceptive. Traditional solutions and the various ideological strategies that put themselves forward as alternatives have not been comprehensive enough in scope. In the most accurate sense of the word, these solutions are not radical enough; they have failed to attack the roots of our problems.

Some continue to view problems individualistically rather than seeing the cancerlike sickness that affects whole systems. Others cling to the belief or hope that our problems can be solved within the structures of present systems and fail to comprehend the need for alternative vision. Still others define everything ideologically and see solutions coming only through their gaining and manipulating political power, which merely perpetuates one of the most central idolatries of the present system. To deal with the root causes of our problems, to begin to offer more comprehensive solutions on the road to meaningful social change, we must deal with the need for basic change in human values and relationships on both personal and corporate levels. Anything less will lead to disillusionment, a sense of futility, and conformity to present historical realities.

I have no confidence that the vision and power for new human values and relationships can be generated from the present system or from its ideological opponents. Christians have that responsibility. Social leadership, in providing alternative vision and values, is a Christian responsibility because the necessary breaks with the mindset of the present system require deep and thoroughgoing transformation and life redirection, which is at the heart of the power of Christ in the world. Fundamental change of this proportion is basic to the claim of the gospel and is outworking in the context of a body of believers committed to Christ and to one another.

But Christians will never provide social leadership so long as they continue to live as the children of this age rather than as the children of God. The body of Christ, as described in the New Testament, is something quite different from Sunday collections of the children of this age. The local community of believers is to *be* Christ in the world and to embody the new order that was brought about by the entrance of Jesus Christ into history.

The common life of Christians as the new community is intended to be an outcropping of a whole new order of things, the first fruits of a new creation, a place where men and women can begin to experience the quality of life God intends for human society. Their life together is to be nothing less than a new society growing up in the shell of the old. Theirs is a life where everything is shared fully and freely—money, possessions, time, decisions, family, work and vocation, deepest hurts and greatest fears, strongest dreams and hopes, joy and sorrow, worship, ethical and political discernment, ministry and active witness in the world, and the healing that God grants to them through their love and trust for one another. The church will not be used as an instrument of God's healing among the nations if we are unable to be vehicles for the healing of one another in our local fellowships.

For the children of God, the ethic of individualism is ended in the New Testament understanding which sees our individuality expressed as various parts of a physical body. That powerful metaphor for the church must be revived in our congregations, where even the thought of it is now so foreign. What is now emerging in many quarters is a new vision of the church in its shared common life, in its presence in a neighborhood community, and in its witness in the world. The vision of the church as a new society is coming to be shared among many Christian communities from a wide variety of theological traditions in this country. One evidence of that spirit came at a Detroit gathering of Christian communities in the fall of 1975. The following resolution was adopted to express their common concerns and commitments:

We believe the action of the Holy Spirit in our day, while including individual conversion and personal renewal, is largely intended to bring about renewal of the church itself as an alien and charismatic society of God's people fully involved in the secular world, and testifying to certain neglected biblical principles as foundational to its renewed corporate life. This testimony proclaims the gospel to necessarily include a vision of the church, the Body of Christ, as an alternate society to the secular order in which it operates with prophetic force.

Resulting from a commitment to this vision, several local congregations (from a variety of theological and social origins) are discovering for themselves radically new lifestyles, new structures of corporate life and leadership, and new types of ministry that stabilize and strengthen their own internal church community while enabling it to serve the needs of their surrounding neighborhoods and the needs of the world.

With these new discoveries proving themselves to be viable expressions of local church life and ministry, there is now emerging a pressing concern for the renewal of the church in its larger dimensions, both denominational and ecumenical.

There is legitimacy to the charge that, for some groups of Christians, community has been an occasion for withdrawal from the world, a means of escaping the responsibilities for Christian witness and action in the world. When this happens, it is a clear sign of disobedience on the part of God's people and an indication that they have again lost touch with their biblical identity. God's purpose in gathering a people together into community is that they might be the vessels and vanguard of his liberating and healing activity in history. Christian community must never mean withdrawal from the world but, on the contrary, is intended to be the very *means* of the church's engagement with the world, the basis and source of all Christian involvement.

Similarly, the style of servanthood is neither a reason for withdrawal from conflict nor an illusive desire for purity. Rather, it is the means that God has chosen in Christ and in the church for the liberation of the world. We are to be servants of God and not slaves to this world. Servanthood can only come from freedom. In order to be free to serve we must first know who we are. Jesus was clear about who he was. His authentic freedom and control over his own life before God enabled him to give himself fully in serving the world. Jesus chose to give his life away, it was not taken from him. While slavery is imposed, servanthood is a choice and originates in freedom. The slavery that is imposed upon the poor, women, blacks, and other oppressed minorities by the social and economic circumstances of their lives must never be confused with servanthood. To counsel the oppressed into passivity is a brutal distortion of the example of Christ's servanthood and ignores the central truth that freedom is the basis of servanthood. Christians must be those who are free before God to serve, who refuse to struggle for power for themselves, but rather struggle to *empower* others who have no freedom. That is the servanthood of Christ, and that is the key to social change for biblical people. The servanthood of biblical people is the very power of God in the world.

The servant community is the gathered style of biblical people. It is the style of those who live as sojourners in the land, and it is the way that God has so mightily used a faithful people in history and will use them again in our own day.

List of Related Books

Berkhof, Hendrik. *Christ and the Powers*. Scottdale, Pa.: Herald Press, 1962.

Bonhoeffer, Dietrich. *Life Together*. New York: Harper & Row, 1954.

————. *Cost of Discipleship*. New York: Macmillan, 1963.

Ellul, Jacques. *Presence of the Kingdom*. New York: Seabury Press, 1967.

————. *The Political Illusion*. New York: Alfred A. Knopf, 1967.

————. *Violence: Reflections from a Christian Perspective*. New York: Seabury Press, 1969.

————. *False Presence of the Kingdom*. New York: Seabury Press, 1972.

Jordan, Clarence. *The Sermon on the Mount*. Valley Forge: Judson Press, 1970.

————. *The Substance of Faith and Other Cotton Patch Sermons*. New York: Association Press, 1972.

Merton, Thomas. *Conjectures of a Guilty Bystander*. Garden City, N.Y.: Doubleday, 1966.

————. *Raids on the Unspeakable*. New York: New Directions, 1970.

————. *Contemplation in a World of Action*. Garden City, N.Y.: Doubleday, 1971.

————. *The Thomas Merton Reader*. Garden City, N.Y.: Doubleday, 1974.

Moltmann, Jürgen. *The Crucified God*. New York: Harper & Row, 1974.

Post-American (recently renamed *Sojourners*). 1029 Vermont Avenue, N.W., Washington, D.C. 20005.

Stringfellow, William. *A Private and Public Faith*. Grand Rapids, Mich.: Eerdmans, 1962.

————. *Free in Obedience*. New York: Seabury Press, 1964.

————. *Suspect Tenderness*. New York: Holt, Rinehart and Winston, 1971.

————. *An Ethic for Christians and Other Aliens in a Strange Land.* Waco, Tex.: Word Books, 1973.

Yoder, John Howard. *The Original Revolution*. Scottdale, Pa.: Herald Press, 1971.

————. *Politics of Jesus*. Grand Rapids, Mich.: Eerdmans, 1972.

Sojourners
formerly the Post American

In the fall of 1971, the *Post-American* emerged to give expression to a fresh spirit growing among a new generation of evangelical Christians. The earliest commitment of the publication was to a radical outworking of biblical faith and life. The *Post-American* quickly became controversial and the subject of much attention despite its smallness; it attracted a loyal readership from a wide cross section of theological traditions and ecclesiastical denominations as it grew from a quarterly tabloid to a monthly magazine.

Beginning as a barb in the conscience of establishment Christianity over issues of war, civil religion, economic and racial oppression, and the church's deep cultural conformity, to becoming a noted forum for the advocacy of new forms of discipleship, community, social action, and biblical political witness, the *Post-American* has developed in range of concern and depth of coverage.

Fundamental to us is the understanding of the church's biblical identity as a new community which is a sign of the kingdom in history, an alien society of God's people whose life and action is intended to play a prophetic and decisive role in the world. That vision of the church was present in embryonic form at our inception and has since grown to be the foundation of the purposes of the magazine, which itself now flows from an active Christian community and is in relationship to many other communities. From the outset, we have felt it was most essential that Christians rediscover their biblical identity and learn to live not as the children of this age but as the children of God.

For those reasons we have chosen *Sojourners* as the new name of the magazine. It is one of the central biblical metaphors for the people

143

of God who are to live in the world as strangers, pilgrims, aliens, and sojourners because of their loyalty to the kingdom of God, because of their identity as those who have entered into a new order of things.

Historically, sojourners was one of the earliest names used to describe the first local Christian congregations; it is derived from the same Greek word from which we get our word "parish." Contrary to the distortions of separatist fundamentalism and other sectarian groups, the biblical instruction to live as sojourners is not an excuse to withdraw from involvement in the world. Rather, it is the style of deep participation in the world that is most crucial and ultimately decisive. It is a way of loving and serving the world without conforming to it. By living as sojourners we are witnesses to the power of the kingdom in history and participate in the revolution of human life and society which is begun and completed by Jesus Christ.

The simple purpose of *Sojourners* will be to serve in the rebuilding of the church by "discerning the times through the life and faith of biblical people."

We have established an active group of contributing editors and a string of correspondents around the country and in various parts of the world to cover events and issues quickly and on location.

Biblical studies, theological analysis and reflection, and historical essays will continue to play a key role in the magazine, but we will be doing more news articles and investigative features, along with reviews of books, films, and the arts. In addition, interviews and profiles of people, communities, and ministries, social and political discernment in editorial comment, and advocacy journalism in support of the poor and oppressed will be major parts of *Sojourners*.

Regular columns will be written by people in the church whom we believe have most to say to us. *Sojourners* will offer brief notes to keep its readers better informed about happenings and events shaping the life of the church, to make them aware of crucial resources, and to share new developments in community, ministry, and public actions growing out of the life of local bodies of Christians.

Basic to the commitment of *Sojourners* is to serve in the building of community at the local church level. The whole magazine will reflect that commitment and will regularly focus on the life and action of a wide variety of Christian communities. This should give practical help in the building of Christian community by sharing the experience of existing communities from a wide variety of theological and social traditions.

Close relationships between a number of communities in this country are developing. *Sojourners* is being asked by many of them to be a voice and visible witness of this growing circle of communities to the wider church and society. At the center of the magazine's readership will be communities, local congregations, and small groups who are seeking to embody the concerns and the commitments of which the publication speaks. *Sojourners*, then, will be calling people not just to ideas, but to a way of life and action that can be seen, experienced, and embraced.

The Christian community is intended to provide alternative vision and social leadership in the world. A publication which chooses a Christian vocation needs to provide such leadership in journalism. There is now a pressing need for a radically biblical presence in American journalism. That is what we feel called to be.

JIM WALLIS, Editor
and STAFF OF SOJOURNERS